# HOW TO OVERCOME A SCARCITY MINDSET AND EMBRACE ABUNDANCE

*Stop Thinking Small and Start Thinking Plenty*

*By Alex Carter*

This book is a work of nonfiction. While the stories shared are inspired by real experiences, some names and identifying details have been changed to protect privacy.

Published by Edenroot Press
edenrootpress.com

EDENROOT
PRESS

# Contents

# Acknowledgements

This book was born from a personal journey, one that moved from fear and limitation to belief and expansion. But I didn't walk that road alone.

To everyone who has ever reminded me that mindset is more powerful than circumstance, thank you. Your words stayed with me longer than you know.

To the readers of my previous books, who continue to share their breakthroughs, stories, and encouragement, you are the reason I keep writing. Your courage to grow inspires mine.

To my mentors, both real and virtual, thank you for modelling abundance not just in theory, but in how you live, give, and lead. Your example lit the path.

To my close friends and family, who've listened, supported, and held space during the creation of this work, you are the foundation of everything I build. Thank you for believing in me, even when I needed to relearn how to believe in myself.

And finally, to *you*, the reader: thank you for showing up for your own growth. Thank you for choosing abundance when it might've felt easier to settle for scarcity. Writing this book for you has been an honour, and I hope reading it becomes part of the legacy you pass on.

Keep thinking big. Keep expanding. The world needs what only you can offer.

With deep gratitude,
**Alex Carter**

---

# About the Author

**Alex Carter** is an internationally recognised wealth mindset coach, financial empowerment speaker, and New York Times bestselling author. With over 20 years of experience in personal finance, entrepreneurship, and personal development, Alex has helped thousands transform their financial futures, not by chasing money, but by mastering their mindset.

From humble beginnings to building multiple streams of income and achieving financial independence, Alex's mission is clear: to help ordinary people create extraordinary financial lives, one powerful decision at a time.

When not writing, Alex can be found hiking with their dog, mentoring young entrepreneurs, or running money mindset workshops in under-resourced communities.

# Introduction: Why Abundance Thinking Changes Everything

*"Whether you think you can, or you think you can't, you're right." – Henry Ford*

---

## The Invisible Cage of Scarcity

Have you ever looked at your bank balance and felt a cold wave of anxiety, even if there was enough in there to get by? Or perhaps you've seen someone else's success and immediately thought, *"They probably had connections... things like that just don't happen to people like me."* If so, you're not alone, and more importantly, you're not broken. What you're experiencing is not a personal flaw. It's a mindset.

A scarcity mindset is like wearing tinted glasses that subtly, but powerfully, distort everything you see. It colours your thoughts, shrinks your confidence, and limits your potential. It tells you there's never enough, time, money, love, opportunity. It whispers that others succeeding means there's less left for you. And perhaps most damaging of all, it convinces you that safety lies in staying small.

But what if that's not true?
 What if everything changes, not when you earn more,

find the perfect job, or win the lottery, but when you choose to *think* differently?

That's the premise of this book, and the power of the **abundance mindset**.

---

## Scarcity vs. Abundance: Two Lenses on the Same World

To understand what's possible, let's start with a clear distinction:

- **Scarcity Mindset**: Believes there's a finite pie. More for someone else means less for you. It's driven by fear, comparison, and survival. It shows up as hoarding, procrastination, perfectionism, and constant anxiety about not having or being enough.

- **Abundance Mindset**: Believes the pie can grow. That opportunities multiply when shared. It's grounded in trust, creativity, and expansion. It shows up as generosity, gratitude, risk-taking, and growth.

Stephen Covey, author of *The 7 Habits of Highly Effective People*, described scarcity thinking as "the zero-sum paradigm of life." If you win, I lose. But with abundance? There's room for us all.

This shift in perspective doesn't just feel better. It *works better*. Because the way you think, about yourself, about money, about the world, directly shapes the outcomes you create. You don't get what you want. You get what you *believe*.

---

## A Real-Life Shift: From Scarcity to Self-Made Success

Let's start with a story, one that shows the power of transforming your mindset.

When Lisa lost her job at 34, she had £200 in her account, two kids, and no partner to lean on. Her first instinct? Panic. She applied to a dozen jobs, most below her skill level, hoping someone, *anyone*, would say yes.

But after weeks of silence and a growing pit of fear, she realised something: her whole approach was driven by desperation. She was thinking small, grasping at scraps. So she made a radical decision. Instead of begging the world to give her something, she asked herself a new question: *What do I have to give?*

She started offering online marketing services from home. The first gig paid £75. But her energy shifted, she showed up with confidence, treated herself like a professional, and dared to pitch bigger clients. Within six months, she was earning more than in her previous job. Two years later, she launched a digital agency that now employs six people.

Lisa didn't win the lottery. She rewired her *mindset*. She stopped thinking like a victim of scarcity and started showing up like the source of abundance.

---

## Your Mindset Is Your Ceiling, Lift It

We all have an invisible ceiling above us, a limit set not by the economy, our upbringing, or even our education, but by our *thinking*. Until you raise that ceiling, you will always bounce back to the same results, no matter how hard you try to push forward.

Here's what abundance thinking does:

- It opens your eyes to opportunities you were blind to before.

- It changes how people perceive and respond to you.

- It builds resilience, so you keep moving even when life throws curveballs.

- It attracts more of what you want, because you're operating from a place of belief, not lack.

That's why this book exists. Not to teach you how to save every penny or hustle non-stop. But to guide you to the source of real wealth: your *mindset*.

---

## What This Book Will Help You Do

Over the next 20 chapters, you'll explore:

- How to identify and dismantle your scarcity scripts

- The science behind abundance and how to rewire your brain

- How abundance shows up in money, career, relationships, and health

- Tools like gratitude, generosity, and identity shifts to reinforce abundance

- Real stories of people who transformed their lives by thinking differently

- Step-by-step strategies to embrace abundance in everyday decisions

Whether you're earning £20,000 or £200,000, whether you're at the start of your journey or reinventing your life after setbacks, abundance is available to you now. But it starts with your thoughts.

This is not just a book. It's a mirror, a toolkit, and a key.

---

## Your First Step

By the end of this book, I want you to believe, truly believe, that you're not at the mercy of your circumstances. You are a powerful creator, and your thoughts are the seeds of your future.

So here's your first step:
Start paying attention to your inner dialogue. Notice when scarcity shows up in your words:

> "I can't afford that."
> "I'm just not cut out for that."
> "That's for other people, not me."
> "Better not try, it'll probably fail."

Don't judge these thoughts. Just see them. Because awareness is the first crack in the ceiling.

## Takeaway

The life you want isn't waiting for perfect conditions.
It's waiting for a new mindset.
A mindset that says:

> *There is more than enough.*
> *I am more than enough.*
> *And I can create a life of plenty, starting*
> *now.*

Let's begin.

# Chapter 1: Recognising the Scarcity Trap

*"The first step toward change is awareness. The second step is acceptance." – Nathaniel Branden*

---

## The Trap You Didn't Know You Were In

Scarcity mindset doesn't show up waving a red flag. It doesn't shout, "Hey! You're living small!" No, it whispers. It disguises itself as caution, practicality, humility. It lurks behind everyday decisions, guiding your thoughts in subtle, restrictive ways. That's what makes it so powerful, and so dangerous.

You might be living in the scarcity trap and not even realise it.

You might:

- Decline opportunities because they feel "too big" or "out of reach"

- Avoid investing in yourself because "it's not the right time"

- Feel discomfort or envy when others succeed

- Hesitate to ask for a raise or charge more for your services

- Constantly say "I can't afford it" or "I'm not ready yet"

On the surface, these thoughts seem rational. But underneath, they're symptoms of a deeper belief: *there's not enough… and I'm not enough.*

Recognising the scarcity trap is the first, and most crucial, step in breaking free from it.

---

## Signs You're Trapped in Scarcity Thinking

Let's dig into some common signs that scarcity might be shaping your reality more than you think:

### 1. You Frequently Feel There's "Never Enough"

Time, money, energy, love, it always feels like you're running on empty. Even when you accomplish something, there's a gnawing sense it's not quite enough. There's no satisfaction, just an endless chase.

### 2. Comparison is Constant

You measure your success against others, and often feel like you're behind. Instead of celebrating others, their wins trigger insecurity. Social media becomes a scoreboard, not inspiration.

### 3. You Hoard Resources (Even Emotionally)

You're afraid to spend money, even when you can afford it. You avoid sharing your ideas or supporting others out of fear they'll get ahead of you. You struggle to trust, believing if you give, you'll be left with less.

### 4. You Play Small

You talk yourself out of going after big goals. You downplay your talents. You aim for "safe" instead of "significant." Why? Because you're afraid there isn't space for you to truly thrive.

### 5. You Default to Worst-Case Thinking

Every opportunity is met with "What if it goes wrong?" instead of "What if it works?" You protect yourself from disappointment by expecting failure before you begin.

Sound familiar? Most people experience some of these patterns. The key isn't to judge yourself, it's to notice. Because until you recognise the scarcity trap, you'll keep repeating it.

---

## Where Scarcity Comes From

Scarcity mindset doesn't just appear one day. It's built layer by layer, shaped by your upbringing, the culture around you, and the economic environment you've lived in. Let's look at some of the most common origins:

## 1. Childhood Conditioning

Did you grow up hearing things like:

- "Money doesn't grow on trees."

- "We can't afford that."

- "Don't ask for too much, be grateful."

Even well-meaning parents pass on beliefs rooted in lack. If your household was focused on survival, stretching every penny, fearing bills, putting dreams on hold, you likely absorbed that mindset. It becomes the lens through which you view the world.

## 2. Cultural Narratives

Many societies reward struggle and self-sacrifice. We glorify the hustle. We romanticise lack, phrases like "starving artist" or "poor but honest" reinforce the idea that wealth is suspect and scarcity is virtuous.

Advertising doesn't help either. It constantly reminds us what we *don't* have, fuelling a sense of inadequacy to sell products.

### 3. Economic Environment

If you've lived through recessions, redundancy, or financial hardship, scarcity thinking can take root as a form of self-protection. You begin to expect loss, to assume the worst, to believe security is a fantasy.

Over time, these patterns stop being circumstantial, they become *internalised*. You don't just experience scarcity. You start to *believe in it*.

---

## How Scarcity Shows Up in Everyday Choices

You don't have to be struggling financially to live with scarcity thinking. It shows up in small, daily decisions that shape your future without you realising it.

- **Declining a growth opportunity** because you fear you're not ready

- **Underpricing your services** because you think people won't pay more

- **Not asking for help** because you believe support is a limited resource

- **Staying in a job that drains you** because you worry there's nothing better

- **Micromanaging your team or family** out of fear things will fall apart without control

It's even in the language you use:

> "I don't have time."
> "I wish I could, but I can't afford it."
> "People like me don't get those chances."
> "I'll never be able to do that."

Every one of those phrases is a belief being reinforced. A story you're telling yourself, often on autopilot.

Scarcity makes you believe you're just being *realistic*. But what's "realistic" is often just what you've gotten used to.

---

## Case Study: The Corporate Climber Who Felt Stuck

Sam was a mid-level manager at a global company. He earned well, had a good team, and a clear path to promotion. But he always played it safe.

When a senior leadership role opened up, he didn't apply. He told himself, "It's not the right time. I should wait until I've ticked every box." But deep down, he feared being rejected, or worse, succeeding and not being able to handle the pressure.

In coaching, Sam uncovered the core belief driving his hesitation: *"If I ask for too much, I'll lose what I already have."* That was a direct echo of his childhood, growing up in a family where ambition was seen as selfish.

Once Sam recognised that belief, he was able to challenge it. He applied for the role, got the job, and now mentors others on abundance-based leadership. His story shows this: scarcity doesn't just affect the struggling, it can sabotage the seemingly "successful" too.

---

## The First Break in the Wall: Awareness

You can't change what you don't see. Awareness is the crack in the scarcity wall, the light seeping through.

So here's your challenge: *Watch your thoughts*. Not to control them, but to become conscious of the ones keeping you small.

Start noticing:

- When you say no to yourself before the world does

- When you tell yourself you're "not ready," "not enough," or "not allowed"

- When fear of loss is stronger than hope for gain

This isn't about guilt or blame. It's about *liberation*. Because once you see the trap, you can choose to leave it.

---

## Try This: The Scarcity Audit

Take 15 minutes today to do a *Scarcity Audit*. Grab a notebook and answer these questions honestly:

1. What do I believe is in short supply in my life?

2. Where do I regularly feel fear or anxiety around not having or being enough?

3. What patterns or habits do I engage in that might stem from scarcity?

4. What did I learn growing up about money, success, and self-worth?

5. Whose voice do I hear in my head when I play small?

Awareness doesn't fix everything. But it gives you the power to make different choices.

---

## Takeaway

The scarcity trap is sneaky. It doesn't always look like struggle, it often wears the mask of "sensible," "humble," or "safe." But if it's holding you back, it's not serving you.

Recognising scarcity thinking is not a sign of weakness, it's a moment of clarity. The moment you stop living on autopilot and start rewriting your story.

Because you were not born to live in lack.
 You were born to expand.

And that expansion begins now, with your awareness.

# Chapter 2: The Science of Abundance

*"Neurons that fire together wire together." – Donald Hebb*

---

## Mindset Isn't Magic, It's Biology

Abundance may sound like a fluffy, feel-good concept. But it's not wishful thinking. It's neuroscience.

Every thought you have, every belief, assumption, or emotional reaction, leaves a physical trace in your brain. Over time, those thoughts form highways: reinforced neural pathways that make certain ways of thinking automatic.

So when you constantly think thoughts like:

> "I'm not enough."
>  "I can't afford that."
>   "Opportunities don't come to people like me."

...your brain wires itself to make those beliefs easier to access and harder to challenge. You're not just *thinking* in scarcity, you're *living* in it at the neurological level.

The good news? You can change it.
 The better news? You're not starting from scratch. Your brain was *designed* to adapt.

Welcome to the science of abundance.

---

## Scarcity Literally Narrows Your Brain

Let's begin with what happens to your brain in a scarcity mindset.

In 2013, researchers Sendhil Mullainathan and Eldar Shafir published a landmark book called *Scarcity: Why Having Too Little Means So Much*. Their research revealed that scarcity, whether it's lack of time, money, or social connection, doesn't just create stress. It reduces your **mental bandwidth**.

Think of it like having 100 units of attention each day. Scarcity eats up 70 just worrying about how to get by. That leaves only 30 units for everything else, solving problems, being creative, making good decisions.

This is called **tunnelling**. Your brain fixates on immediate needs and loses perspective on the bigger picture. You become reactive rather than strategic.

That's why people stuck in financial scarcity often make short-term decisions that hurt them long-term (e.g., payday loans, avoiding investments). The brain isn't "bad with money", it's overloaded.

This applies beyond finances. Scarcity of time leads to burnout. Scarcity of love leads to clinginess or emotional shutdown. In every case, your brain is so focused on what's missing, it can't see what's possible.

---

## Abundance Expands Your Awareness

Now flip the script.

When you shift to abundance thinking, your brain begins to operate differently. Instead of being locked in survival mode, it opens up to creativity, problem-solving, and possibility.

Psychologist Barbara Fredrickson's *Broaden-and-Build Theory* explains this beautifully. Positive emotions (like gratitude, optimism, generosity) broaden your perception and build lasting psychological resources.

In other words, abundance literally helps you **see more**, more options, more solutions, more reasons to act.

It's not just theory. MRI scans show that gratitude activates areas of the brain associated with reward, empathy, and decision-making. Visualisation of positive future outcomes stimulates the prefrontal cortex, your

CEO brain, helping you make choices aligned with long-term success.

Think of it this way:

- **Scarcity = Brain in survival mode**

- **Abundance = Brain in growth mode**

One is reactive and limited. The other is proactive and expansive.

---

## The Mindset-Perception Loop

Here's where things get fascinating. Your brain is wired to filter information based on your beliefs. This is called **confirmation bias**, the tendency to notice and remember what aligns with what you already think.

So if you believe:

> "Money is hard to come by."
> You'll notice every price increase, every rejected job application, every expense that sets you back.

But if you start believing:

"Opportunities are everywhere."
You'll begin to notice chance conversations, potential side hustles, generous offers, creative solutions.

Your beliefs *train* your attention. Your attention *reinforces* your beliefs. That's the mindset-perception loop.

Changing your mindset doesn't mean ignoring reality. It means **shifting your filter** so you can see a broader reality, and act accordingly.

---

## You Can Literally Rewire Your Brain

Now to the most empowering truth in this chapter:
Your brain is not fixed. It's plastic.

**Neuroplasticity** is the brain's ability to reorganise itself by forming new neural connections throughout life. Every new habit, thought pattern, or emotional response you practise rewires your brain's circuitry.

This isn't pseudo-science, it's well-documented.

In one famous study at the University of London, taxi drivers who had to memorise the city's complex streets showed significant growth in their hippocampus, the area responsible for spatial memory.

In another, people who simply *imagined* playing the piano showed similar brain activation to those who actually played it.

What does that mean for you?

It means that practising abundance thinking, gratitude, visualisation, positive reframing, affirmations, generous acts, can **change the structure and function** of your brain. Repeated consistently, these practices form new default patterns.

In short: You are not stuck. You are rewritable.

---

## Mindset Interventions That Work

If you want to rewire your brain for abundance, here are science-backed techniques to start with:

### 1. Gratitude Journaling

Spend 5 minutes each day writing 3 things you're genuinely grateful for. This simple act has been shown to increase optimism, reduce anxiety, and activate reward centres in the brain.

### 2. Visualisation and Scripting

Close your eyes and vividly imagine your abundant future, how it feels, looks, sounds. Pair this with scripting: write a page describing your ideal life as if it's already happening. This activates your brain's reticular activating system (RAS), training it to spot alignment in the real world.

### 3. Reframing Scarcity Language

Every time you catch yourself saying "I can't afford that," shift to: "How *could* I afford that?"
 Or replace "That's too risky" with "What's the potential upside?"
 Language rewires thinking.

### 4. Acts of Generosity

Doing something kind without expecting return boosts dopamine and builds abundance wiring. It proves to your brain: *I have enough to give.* And that changes how you see yourself.

### 5. Affirmations That Align with Identity

Instead of generic mantras, use statements grounded in evidence and action:

> "Every day, I take steps to expand my capacity and attract opportunity."
>  This helps create congruence between belief and behaviour.

## Real-World Proof: Mindset Training in Action

A 2019 Stanford study worked with students from underprivileged backgrounds who had been labelled "at risk." Rather than giving them more tutoring, researchers gave them mindset coaching, teaching them how to reframe failure, use affirmations, and visualise success.

The result? A dramatic improvement in performance, confidence, and long-term outcomes.

In another study, unemployed adults were taught abundance practices, gratitude, goal-setting, reframing, and showed higher re-employment rates than control groups.

Why? Because they approached opportunities differently. They made different choices. They *became* different.

This is the essence of abundance science: **change your brain, change your life**.

---

## Takeaway

Abundance is not wishful thinking, it's brain training. Scarcity shrinks your awareness. Abundance expands

it.
 You don't have to force yourself to "think positive."
 You can *build* an abundant brain through small, daily
shifts that change your wiring over time.

Your mindset isn't just how you feel, it's how your brain
works.
 And the most powerful thing about that?
 You're the one holding the remote.

Let's move forward, deliberately, intelligently, and with
the science on your side.

# Chapter 3: The Cost of Scarcity Thinking

*"You can't live a full life on an empty mindset." –*
*Unknown*

---

## The Hidden Price of Thinking Small

When people think of scarcity, they often think of bank accounts. Of not having "enough" money to buy, build, or become what they want.

But scarcity costs far more than cash.

It affects your emotional health.
It limits your relationships.
It shrinks your dreams.
It makes you protect what you have instead of pursuing what you *could* have.

And the worst part?
You often don't realise what it's stealing from you, until it's already taken too much.

This chapter is your wake-up call. Not to scare you, but to make the cost of staying small impossible to ignore.

Because the truth is: scarcity doesn't just affect your *wallet*. It drains your *life*.

## The Emotional Toll: Fear, Anxiety, and Comparison

Let's start with what scarcity does to your inner world. These costs often go unnoticed, but they're debilitating.

**1. Chronic Fear**

Scarcity thinking keeps you in a constant state of *what if?*

- What if I run out of money?

- What if I make the wrong choice?

- What if they leave me?

- What if I try and fail?

This low-grade fear becomes the background noise of your life. It's exhausting, and it narrows your courage to take action.

**2. Anxiety and Paralysis**

When you believe you don't have enough, time, talent, energy, you become paralysed by indecision. You second-guess every choice. You obsess over getting it perfect. You avoid taking risks, even smart ones. In the end, you waste more than you save.

### 3. Envy and Comparison

Scarcity makes you see others as competition. Their success feels like your failure. Instead of celebrating their wins, you feel like there's less space for you. And over time, that constant comparison erodes your confidence and connection with others.

> Scarcity convinces you that life is a race you're losing, when in fact, it's not a race at all.

---

## The Financial Cost: Playing Not to Lose

Ironically, scarcity doesn't make you *better* with money. It often makes you worse.

Here's how:

### 1. Risk Aversion

You cling to what feels "safe," even if it's limiting. You might stay in an underpaying job for years because you're afraid to leap. Or you avoid starting a side business because failure feels too costly. But here's the twist: *safety often comes at the expense of growth.*

## 2. Underspending on Value

You hesitate to invest in yourself, courses, mentorship, tools, because you see spending as loss, not leverage. You may say, "I can't afford that," but often, the real cost is the opportunity you never gave yourself.

## 3. Under-Earning

Scarcity shows up in what you believe you're worth. You might not negotiate a salary. You might undercharge clients. You might work for "exposure" instead of fair pay. Not because you lack skill, but because you've internalised the belief: *I'm lucky to be here at all.*

A scarcity mindset will have you working twice as hard for half as much, because it keeps you stuck in survival mode, not strategic growth.

---

# The Relationship Cost: Scarcity in Love and Friendship

It's easy to assume scarcity only affects finances. But its claws reach deep into your relationships, too.

## 1. Emotional Hoarding

You hold back vulnerability, affection, praise, because deep down, you believe giving too much might leave you empty or exposed. Scarcity tells you to protect your heart at all costs.

**2. Jealousy and Control**

When you believe love, attention, or loyalty are limited, you become possessive. You may struggle when your partner succeeds, or when a friend finds new connections. Scarcity creates a zero-sum game in relationships, and it breeds resentment.

**3. Competition Instead of Collaboration**

You feel threatened by others' progress. Instead of asking, "How can we grow together?" you think, "What if they get ahead of me?" This mindset erodes trust and leads to isolation, even in the most intimate relationships.

> Scarcity doesn't just make you lonely. It convinces you you're better off that way.

---

## The Opportunity Cost: The Success You Never Saw

Now we come to the most painful cost of all: the life you never lived because you thought it was out of reach.

Scarcity doesn't just steal from your present.
It robs your *future*.

**Meet Jordan: The Talented But Timid Coach**

Jordan had a gift. He was a brilliant mindset coach, helping people overcome fear and self-doubt. His clients raved about him. But Jordan had one major block: he didn't believe he deserved more.

When friends urged him to launch a group programme, he hesitated. "People won't pay for that. I'm not ready. I need more credentials." So he stayed in the comfort of one-on-one work, charging modest fees and burning himself out.

Eventually, his confidence dropped, not because of failure, but because of stagnation. He wasn't growing. He was surviving.

It took a breakdown, exhaustion, tears, and a cancelled client roster, for him to finally admit it: *Scarcity was running the show.*

When he rewrote that belief, started charging what he was worth, launched his programme, and built a team, his income tripled in 12 months.

But what hurt most wasn't the money he hadn't earned. It was the years of potential he had unknowingly abandoned.

---

## Scarcity Shrinks Your Life

Let's get brutally honest.

Scarcity makes you:

- Set smaller goals

- Take fewer chances

- Say no to yourself

- Sabotage your joy

- Feel guilty for wanting more

- See the world as a threat

- Delay your dreams until "someday"

And "someday" rarely comes.

Scarcity doesn't shout. It whispers. It sneaks in. It makes you settle. It convinces you that the safest path is the one where you stay exactly where you are.

But the longer you live in that mindset, the more you pay.

And here's the worst part: *you don't just lose money, you lose momentum, meaning, and magic.*

## Reflection: What Has Scarcity Cost You?

Take a moment, grab your journal, and ask yourself
honestly:

1. Where have I played small because I was afraid
   of not having or being enough?

2. What opportunities have I declined, avoided, or
   ignored due to fear?

3. In what relationships have I held back out of
   insecurity or control?

4. What is the emotional cost of constantly worrying
   about "what if I run out"?

No shame. Just clarity.

Awareness isn't about punishment. It's about reclaiming
your power.

---

## Takeaway

Scarcity thinking is expensive.
It costs you emotionally, financially, and relationally.
It robs your courage.

It shrinks your world.
It delays your future.

And worst of all?
It feels *normal* when you've lived in it long enough.

But now you know better.
And when you know the cost, you can start choosing differently.

Abundance isn't about having more.
It's about *being* more, so you can *do* more and *give* more.

You've paid enough already.
It's time to move in a new direction.

# Chapter 4: Decoding Abundance

*"Abundance is not something we acquire. It is something we tune into." – Wayne Dyer*

---

## Redefining What It Means to Live Abundantly

When most people hear the word *abundance*, they immediately think of money. Overflowing bank accounts. Luxury lifestyles. Expensive holidays. Shiny cars.

But that's not abundance.
 That's *wealth*, and even then, only one narrow version of it.

You can be rich and still live in scarcity. You can have millions and constantly feel like it's not enough, that someone else is winning, that you're just one mistake away from losing it all.

Abundance is something different.
 Something deeper.
 Something quieter but infinitely more powerful.

Abundance is not a *number* in your account.
 It's a *state of being* in your mind, your body, and your choices.

It's not just about *having more*, it's about *being more*.

And once you understand that, you start to see abundance *everywhere*.

---

## Abundance Is a Way of Seeing the World

At its core, abundance is a mindset. A perspective. A lens.

It's the belief that:

- There is more than enough to go around.

- You are not in competition with the world, you are a contributor to it.

- There are always opportunities to grow, love, earn, give, and create.

- Life is working *with* you, not against you.

This perspective changes how you approach every area of life. And once you adopt it, you begin to notice a truth that scarcity hides: **you're already richer than you think**.

Let's break down what abundance really looks like, beyond just money.

## Abundance in Health

True wealth starts in the body.

An abundant person treats their health not as a burden, but as an *asset*. They fuel it, prioritise it, listen to it.

You don't need a gym membership or a private chef to feel abundant in your health. Abundance here looks like:

- Taking time to rest without guilt

- Nourishing your body with food that energises you

- Moving because it feels good, not as punishment

- Tuning in to your energy and honouring your limits

- Feeling strong, capable, and proud of the body you live in

Someone in scarcity sees self-care as indulgent.
Someone in abundance sees it as *essential*.

## Abundance in Time

Scarcity whispers, "There's never enough time."
Abundance says, "I choose how I spend my time."

Time abundance doesn't mean you're always free, it
means you feel *empowered* in how you use your hours.

It means:

- Saying no to things that drain you

- Creating white space in your calendar

- Focusing on what matters, not just what's urgent

- Letting go of the rush and choosing presence

- Trusting that the right pace brings the right
  results

Ever noticed how some people seem calm even with
packed schedules? That's time abundance. It's a
mindset of *ownership*, not lack.

---

## Abundance in Relationships

Scarcity makes you guarded.
 Abundance makes you generous, with love, trust, attention.

In relationships, abundance looks like:

- Celebrating others without comparison

- Sharing your wins and challenges openly

- Believing there's enough love, attention, and connection for all

- Letting others shine without feeling dimmed

- Practicing forgiveness and curiosity, not control

Abundant people don't hoard love. They *give it freely*, knowing that real connection multiplies when shared.

---

## Abundance in Creativity and Purpose

Abundance says, "There's always another idea. Another path. Another chance."

Scarcity says, "What if this is my only shot?"

In your creative or professional life, abundance shows up as:

- Trusting your ideas have value

- Creating without waiting for perfection

- Sharing your voice, even when you feel nervous

- Believing that failure is feedback, not final

- Knowing that you can reinvent yourself at any time

This is how people write books in their sixties, launch businesses after redundancy, or find new purpose after divorce. They believe there's still *more* ahead.

---

## The Difference Between "Having More" and "Being More"

This distinction is everything.

- **Scarcity** says you'll feel better once you *have more*, more money, followers, degrees, validation.

- **Abundance** says you'll feel better once you *become more*, more generous, courageous, loving, free.

One path is chasing. The other is *creating*.

One depends on external conditions. The other is fully within your control.

It's not that wealth, success, and status are wrong. It's that they're incomplete. When you build abundance from the inside, you gain something far more powerful than possessions: *peace*.

---

## Real-Life Examples of Everyday Abundance

Let's look at a few profiles of people who live abundantly, without needing extreme wealth.

### Anita, the Generous Teacher

Anita teaches secondary school in a small town. She doesn't earn six figures. She doesn't own property. But she is deeply abundant.

She mentors younger staff without being asked. She brings fresh fruit to her classroom for pupils who haven't eaten. She starts every morning journaling three things she's grateful for.

People often say she glows. Her secret?

> "I always focus on what I can give, not what I lack."

### Marcus, the Time-Rich Creative

Marcus is a freelance designer. He could take on more work, but he doesn't. He values freedom more than hustle. He blocks off Fridays for personal projects, gardening, and walks with his dog.

He's not interested in growing fast. He's interested in growing *deep*.
His motto: "I'd rather feel full than be full-on."

### Farah, the Community Builder

Farah runs a local café, not to get rich, but to create connection. She hosts free workshops, open mic nights, and community breakfasts. Her income is modest, but her impact is massive.

Abundance for Farah isn't about scaling. It's about *serving*.

> "Every time I give something away, time, energy, kindness, it comes back double."

None of these people are wealthy in the traditional sense. But they all live abundantly. Why? Because they *choose* to.

---

## You Already Have More Than You Think

Here's the truth scarcity hides:

- If you can read this, you have access to learning.

- If you have people who love you, you have wealth.

- If you can take a breath, dream a dream, take a step, you have power.

Abundance starts when you stop chasing *more* and start recognising what you already *have*.

That doesn't mean you stop growing. It means you stop growing from a place of panic, and start growing from a place of *peace*.

---

## Reflection: Where Do You Already Have Abundance?

Take five minutes and answer these:

1. What do I have in abundance right now?

2. Where am I richer than I've given myself credit for?

3. Which area of life could I bring more attention to, health, time, relationships, creativity?

4. What would it look like to *feel* abundant today, without needing anything to change?

Write freely. Let it surprise you.

---

## Takeaway

Abundance isn't a destination.
 It's not about one day "making it."
 It's about *waking up*, to what's already here, and who you already are.

When you stop measuring life only by what you own, and start valuing how you live, love, give, and grow, *that's* abundance.

And that version of success? It's available to you right now.

You don't need to earn more to begin.
 You need to *see differently*.

# Chapter 5: Unlearning Limiting Beliefs

*"We don't see things as they are; we see them as we are." – Anaïs Nin*

---

## Your Beliefs Are the Blueprint

Take a moment to consider this:
 The life you're living today is built on beliefs you didn't consciously choose.

From the way you think about money, to how you define success, to what you think you deserve, it's all been shaped by a set of scripts you absorbed from childhood, culture, school, society.

And unless you *interrupt* those scripts, they run the show. Quietly. Relentlessly. Repetitively.

You don't need more hustle.
 You need a belief upgrade.

Because if your internal blueprint is rooted in scarcity, no amount of effort will get you the results you want. You'll keep sabotaging, shrinking, settling. Not because you're lazy, but because your beliefs are dragging you back down to the level they say is "safe."

It's time to bring those hidden beliefs into the light, and start rewriting them for good.

---

## What Did You Learn About Money and Success?

Most of us never sat down and decided what we believe about money.
We *inherited* it.

Your early experiences, what you saw, heard, and felt growing up, formed your financial identity long before you earned your first pound.

Let's explore some of the most common inherited beliefs:

- "Money doesn't grow on trees."

- "Rich people are greedy."

- "You have to work hard to earn anything."

- "We can't afford that."

- "People like us don't get ahead."

- "Wanting more is selfish."

- "Better safe than sorry."

At the time, these statements may have seemed like wisdom. But many of them were actually rooted in *fear, limitation, and generational struggle.*

They weren't truths.
 They were *coping mechanisms*, passed down by people doing the best they could with what they knew.

But if you never question them, you become the next link in the scarcity chain.

---

## How to Identify Your Scarcity Scripts

If you want to change your life, start by changing the story you're telling yourself.

Here are five powerful prompts to help you uncover your unconscious beliefs:

1. **Growing up, money was…**
   (Stressful? Secretive? Scarce? A source of pride? A cause of conflict?)

2. **People who are wealthy are…**
   (Greedy? Lucky? Smart? Dishonest? Powerful? Generous?)

3. **Success means...**
   (Sacrifice? Status? Security? Pressure? Fulfilment?)

4. **If I had more money, I would...**
   (Feel safer? Be judged? Be freer? Lose friends?)

5. **What I really believe about money is...**
   (Complete this sentence freely, without trying to sound "correct.")

What you write down may surprise you. But that's the point. These beliefs aren't always logical, they're *emotional*. And they've been shaping your choices for decades.

---

## Challenging the "There's Never Enough" Narrative

Scarcity has a soundtrack. And most of us have been playing it on loop for years:

> "There's not enough time."
> "I can't afford it."
> "If I take a risk, I'll lose everything."
> "Who am I to want more?"
> "If they win, I lose."

These aren't harmless phrases. They're *mental contracts*, agreements you've made with limitation.

So let's challenge them.

For every scarcity script, ask:

- Is this always true?

- Who taught me this?

- What evidence do I have to the contrary?

- What would I believe if I had grown up in an abundant household?

Example:

> **Scarcity Script:** "You have to work hard to make money."
> **Challenge:** Is that always true? Are there people who earn passively, or who get paid for their creativity or strategy?
> **Reframe:** "Smart, aligned action earns me money, effort does not equal worth."

The goal here is not to shame your past beliefs, it's to *upgrade them*.

# Rewrite the Script: Replacing Limiting Beliefs

Once you've spotted your old beliefs and challenged their authority, it's time to choose new ones.

Here's how to build empowering abundance-based beliefs:

## 1. Keep Them Present and Personal

Say "I am" or "I believe" statements, not vague affirmations.

> "I am open to receiving wealth in aligned ways."
> "I trust that opportunities are everywhere."
> "I believe in creating value and being well-compensated for it."

## 2. Make Them Believable

Your brain will reject affirmations that feel wildly untrue. So start with bridge beliefs.

Instead of: "I am a millionaire."
Try: "I am learning to think like someone who creates wealth."

Instead of: "Money flows to me effortlessly."
Try: "I am discovering new ways to earn and receive money with ease."

### 3. Anchor Them in Action

Pair your new belief with a behaviour that reinforces it.

- Believe you're worthy of high-paying clients? Raise your rates.

- Believe you can learn new skills? Take a course.

- Believe there's always more time? Say no to something draining.

Every action aligned with abundance strengthens the new belief. Every moment of courage becomes evidence for your brain to rewire.

---

## Case Study: From "Just Getting By" to Financial Expansion

Let me introduce you to Alisha, a freelance writer who lived by one mantra: *"As long as I can get by, I'm doing fine."*

She'd grown up in a household where bills were paid last-minute, money was a constant source of tension, and her parents praised her for not asking for much.

So in adulthood, she kept herself small. She undercharged, over-delivered, and never dreamed bigger than her next rent payment.

In coaching, we unpacked her belief:

> "Wanting more means I'm ungrateful.
> Staying small keeps me safe."

When she saw that belief clearly, really *saw* it, she cried. Because for the first time, she realised it wasn't hers. It was inherited. And it was no longer serving her.

She began journaling daily around a new truth:

> "It's safe for me to grow. I can want more
> *and* be grateful for what I have."

Within six months, she tripled her income. Not by hustling more, but by owning her value, raising her rates, and working with clients who respected her worth.

Her external life changed, but the real transformation? It was internal.
She stopped playing the "just enough" game, and started living in *possibility*.

---

## Your Beliefs Shape Your Reality

Beliefs are not just ideas. They are instructions.

They tell your brain what to notice, your heart what to feel, and your hands what to do.

- Believe life is a struggle? You'll find proof of that.

- Believe people can't be trusted? You'll subconsciously push them away.

- Believe there's not enough? You'll hoard, hesitate, and hide.

But when you believe:

> "There's more where that came from."
> "I am safe to expand."
> "Money flows to me when I create value."
> "There's enough success to go around."
> "I am worthy of more."

Everything changes.

Not overnight. But inevitably.

---

## Reflection: Rewrite One Belief Today

Pick one old belief you want to retire. Then write:

1. The old belief

2. The evidence it's not always true

3. The new belief you're choosing

4. One small action to reinforce it today

Example:

- Old: "I'm not good with money."

- Evidence: "I've paid off debt, saved before, made smart purchases."

- New: "I'm becoming more financially confident every day."

- Action: "I'll spend 10 minutes reviewing my finances with curiosity, not fear."

---

## Takeaway

You are not your past.
You are not your parents' fears.
You are not your culture's limitations.
You are not your scarcity scripts.

You are the author now.

And the pen is in your hands.

Write something new. Write something bold.
 Write a story rooted in belief, expansion, and possibility.

Because when you change your beliefs, you change
your entire life.

# Chapter 6: Building an Abundance Identity

*"You can't outperform your self-image. You'll always return to who you believe you are." – Alex Carter*

---

## The Most Important Person You'll Ever Believe In

Before money flows, before opportunities open, before others recognise your value, *you* must.

Because the world can only mirror back to you what you believe about yourself.

This isn't about arrogance or pretending. It's about stepping into an identity that says:

> *I am more than enough.*
> *I create value.*
> *I deserve to thrive.*
> *I am capable of creating abundance in my life.*

Scarcity identity sounds like:

- "I'm just not that kind of person."

- "People like me don't get rich."

- "I'm not the confident type."

- "I'll never be as good as them."

It's subtle. It's believable. And it's deeply limiting.

Abundance identity, on the other hand, is expansive. It's not about what you have. It's about *who you're becoming.*

And if you want to live abundantly, you need to think, act, and *see yourself* through a new lens.

---

## From "Not Enough" to "More Than Enough"

Let's talk about your self-concept.

This is the mental portrait you hold of yourself, your qualities, limits, talents, and potential. It determines how you show up in the world, what you tolerate, what you pursue, and what you believe is "for people like you."

Here's the truth:

> You will never out-earn, out-create, or outlive your self-image.

If you see yourself as someone who always struggles, you'll find ways to struggle, even with money in the bank.

If you believe you're the supporting act, not the main event, you'll keep handing the mic to others.

If you think you're destined for "just enough," then "more than enough" will feel uncomfortable, maybe even unsafe.

But here's the good news: **your identity is not fixed**. It can be *designed*.

You get to decide who you are now, and who you're becoming next.

---

## The Role of Self-Worth in Abundance

Self-worth is not about thinking you're better than anyone else. It's knowing, deep down, that you are inherently valuable, not because of what you *do*, but because of who you *are*.

When you anchor into high self-worth, everything changes:

- You stop begging for crumbs and start setting standards.

- You stop chasing validation and start building value.

- You stop playing small and start taking up space.

Here's the link:

> High self-worth supports abundant thinking.
> Low self-worth fuels scarcity.

If you don't believe you're worthy of good things, your brain will reject opportunities, even when they're right in front of you. It will downplay your wins, sabotage your growth, and keep you stuck in cycles of "almost."

This is why many people don't have a *money* problem. They have a *self-worth* problem.

---

## Crafting a New Identity: Three Tools That Work

So how do you build an abundance identity? You use tools that train your mind to see yourself, and your future, differently.

### 1. Affirmations That Reflect Who You're Becoming

Affirmations aren't magic words. They're mental conditioning.

When done right, they interrupt the inner critic and reinforce the identity you're choosing to embody.

Use statements that are:

- Present tense

- Emotionally resonant

- Believable and specific

Examples:

- "I am creating a life of freedom and choice."

- "I trust myself to make decisions that align with abundance."

- "I am worthy of receiving, not just surviving."

- "I show up like the successful version of me, even before the results."

Say them daily, ideally aloud, and with emotion. Repetition builds wiring. Emotion cements it.

### 2. Visualisation: Becoming It Before You See It

Athletes use this. Top performers use this. Abundant thinkers use this.

Visualisation is not daydreaming, it's mental rehearsal. It primes your brain to act in alignment with your desired identity.

Here's a 5-minute daily practice:

- Close your eyes.

- Picture your abundant self going about your day.

- What do they wear? How do they speak? What choices do they make?

- Feel it. Embody it. Then act from that version of you today.

Your brain doesn't fully distinguish between imagined and real experiences. This means visualisation literally creates new neural pathways, fast-tracking belief and behaviour change.

### 3. Identity Anchoring: Linking Belief to Behaviour

To lock in your new identity, anchor it to small daily actions.

For example:

- Want to be someone who values your time? Block your calendar and say no more often.

- Want to be someone who owns their expertise? Start sharing insights publicly, even if you feel nervous.

- Want to be someone who receives money confidently? Practise saying, "I charge £X for my work" with conviction.

The goal isn't to fake it. It's to *practice being it*, until it feels natural.

---

## Real-World Examples: Embodying Abundance Before the Results

### Michelle Obama: Acting Like She Belonged

Before Michelle Obama was First Lady, she was a working-class girl from Chicago's South Side. In her memoir *Becoming*, she shared how she often felt like she didn't belong in elite rooms.

But instead of shrinking, she trained herself to stand tall, even when her knees were shaking.

She said, "Failure is a feeling long before it becomes an actual result... it's vulnerability that breeds self-doubt."

She learned to embody poise and presence *before* she had public recognition. That's abundance identity in action.

**Lewis Hamilton: Visualising Victory**

Formula One world champion Lewis Hamilton has spoken openly about visualising his wins before they happened. As a teenager with limited resources, he'd mentally rehearse standing on the podium.

He didn't wait to feel like a champion, he *became* one in his mind first. The results followed.

These stories prove a powerful truth:

> Identity comes before outcome.
>  You don't wait to *become* someone, you *decide*.

---

## Reflection: Who Are You Becoming?

Take a few minutes and journal your answers to these:

1. What identity am I currently living from? (Be honest.)

2. What beliefs, habits, or self-talk reflect that identity?

3. Who am I choosing to become next?

4. How does that version of me act, speak, and make decisions?

5. What is one small way I can practise *being* that person today?

This is how you upgrade your self-image: not in one big leap, but in daily choices that align with your vision.

---

## Takeaway

You don't need to wait for the money, the job, the partner, or the external validation to feel like "enough."

You can choose that identity now.
And when you do, everything begins to rise to meet it.

Because abundance doesn't come to who you *were*.
It flows through who you *believe you are* becoming.

So ask yourself:

What would the abundant version of me do today?

Then do that.

And repeat. Until it becomes you.

# Chapter 7: Rewriting Your Money Story

*"Money is not just coins and notes. It's a mirror of your mindset." – Alex Carter*

---

## What's the Story You've Been Telling Yourself?

Every one of us has a *money story*, a narrative running in the background that shapes how we earn, spend, save, give, and think about money.

And here's the thing: most people never write this story intentionally.
 They inherit it.

You might be living by a script you didn't choose, one written years ago by your parents, your environment, or your culture. A script that sounds like:

> "Money is hard to come by."
>  "I'll never be wealthy unless I win the lottery."
> "If I get rich, people will judge me."
> "It's safer to keep my head down."
> "I'm just not good with money."

Left unchallenged, these stories dictate how far you go.
They become self-fulfilling prophecies.
 But here's the truth:

> You can't create a wealthy life from a story
> of lack.

If you want financial freedom, you have to start by
rewriting the story you're telling yourself about money.

Because your money story isn't just about numbers, it's
about *identity, belief, and possibility*.

---

## The Most Common Scarcity-Based Money Stories

Let's decode some of the most common money stories
rooted in scarcity. You may recognise more than one:

### 1. The "Not Enough" Story

> *"There's never enough to go around."*

This is the most widespread scarcity script. It leads to
hoarding, chronic under-earning, and fear-based
decisions. Even when money is present, it feels like it
could disappear any second.

### 2. The "Money is Dirty" Story

*"Wealthy people are greedy or selfish."*

This belief creates inner conflict, because even if you want more money, you subconsciously associate it with negative traits. As a result, you repel wealth or sabotage it when it comes.

### 3. The "Struggle = Worth" Story

*"You have to work really hard to deserve money."*

This script glorifies overwork and guilt around ease. It blocks passive income, smart delegation, and the idea of earning more by working *smarter*.

### 4. The "I'm Bad with Money" Story

*"I'm just not the kind of person who manages money well."*

This belief becomes a convenient excuse to avoid growth. It prevents financial education and reinforces a sense of helplessness around numbers, budgeting, and investing.

### 5. The "Better Safe Than Wealthy" Story

*"Stick with what you've got. Don't rock the boat."*

This narrative glorifies stability over expansion. It leads people to stay in jobs they hate, undercharge for their services, or avoid new income streams, even when opportunities are knocking.

---

## Step One: Identify *Your* Personal Money Narrative

You can't rewrite what you haven't read. So let's bring your current money story into the light.

Ask yourself the following:

- Growing up, what did I learn about money?

- How did my parents or caregivers talk about it?

- What feelings come up when I think about wealth, guilt, excitement, shame, fear?

- When I imagine myself being truly financially free, what voices pop up? ("That's unrealistic." "You don't need that much." "Who do you think you are?")

- How do I behave with money, do I avoid it, obsess over it, overspend, underspend?

These reflections will show you the script running the show. Don't rush this process. Write freely, honestly, and without judgement.

What you'll often find is that your money story *makes perfect sense*, given your history.
But that doesn't mean it has to be your *future*.

---

## Step Two: Choose a New Money Story

This is where the magic begins.

You are not locked into your past. You are the *author* now.

Here's how to rewrite your financial narrative into one that supports abundance:

### 1. Flip the Limiting Belief

Old story: *"There's never enough."*
New story: *"I always find a way to generate and receive more than I need."*

Old story: *"I'm bad with money."*
New story: *"I'm learning to be an excellent steward of my finances."*

Old story: *"Wanting more is selfish."*
New story: *"The more I have, the more I can give."*

Start with your current belief. Then write a new one that feels *empowering and believable*. Not a fantasy, but a vision of who you're becoming.

## 2. Write a Money Manifesto

Take 15 minutes to write a one-page letter that starts with:

> *"Here's what I now believe about money..."*

Describe how money flows to you, how you use it, how you feel about receiving and giving it, and what kind of impact you create with it.

Write in the present tense. Be bold. Be unapologetic.

This is your new story. Come back to it often.

## 3. Find Evidence That It's Possible

Your brain needs proof. So go find it.

- Look for people like you who have transformed their finances.

- Read success stories.

- Track your own small wins, raising your rates, making a new investment, receiving unexpected money.

- Celebrate them all. These are plot points in your new chapter.

---

## Case Study: Two Entrepreneurs, Two Stories

### Sophie – The Overgiver

Sophie was a wellness coach who gave her clients everything, hour-long calls, personalised plans, even late-night texts. She charged £45 per session and felt guilty even asking for that.

Why? Her story: *"Helping people shouldn't be about money."*

But beneath that was fear: *"If I charge more, they'll leave. I'm not really worth it."*

After working on her money mindset, Sophie raised her rates to £120, created a group programme, and set boundaries. Her income doubled in six months, and her clients got *better* results. Why? Because she showed up as someone who valued her work.

Her new story:

> "I create immense value, and money flows to me when I do."

### Nathan – The Corporate Escapee

Nathan worked in finance. He earned well, but always felt anxious. He never trusted the money would last. He had grown up in a family where saving every penny was survival.

Even with a six-figure salary, he hoarded rather than invested. He stayed in a job he hated for "security." Until burnout forced a change.

In therapy, he realised his story:

> "If I stop playing it safe, I'll lose everything."

He rewrote it to:

> "I am the creator of safety and success, my ideas are my assets."

Today, Nathan runs his own consultancy. He invests with confidence. And for the first time, he feels *free*.

---

## Reflection: Draft Your New Financial Identity

Use the prompts below to craft your new money story:

1. *The old story I'm letting go of is...*

2.  *This story kept me safe by...*

3.  *But now, I choose to believe...*

4.  *My new money story is...*

5.  *One way I'll live this new story today is...*

Repeat this practice often. Your identity around money, like anything else, is formed through repetition and action.

---

## Takeaway

You are not broken.
You're just following an old story.

But stories can be rewritten.
Characters can evolve.
And you, *you*, are the author of what comes next.

You don't need to wait for your bank balance to change.
You need to change your beliefs, your words, and your behaviour.

Because the richest people are not the ones who inherited wealth.
They're the ones who rewrote the script.

You can, too.

# Chapter 8: Practising Gratitude as an Abundance Accelerator

*"Gratitude turns what we have into enough, and more."*
*– Melody Beattie*

---

## The Fastest Path to Abundance

If I told you there was one habit that could:

- Improve your physical health

- Strengthen your relationships

- Reduce anxiety and depression

- Increase resilience and optimism

- Expand your capacity to create wealth

…would you do it?

Here's the thing, such a habit exists. And it's not a secret. It's not complicated. It doesn't require fancy training or expensive tools.

It's **gratitude**.

Gratitude is one of the most powerful mindset tools available.
It costs nothing.
Takes minutes.
And delivers life-changing returns.

More than just good manners or polite thank-yous, gratitude is an *energetic frequency*, a *mental habit*, and a *practical tool* that opens the door to abundance, quickly.

Because when you feel grateful, you're not just noticing what you have.
You're *training your brain* to see and receive more.

---

## The Neuroscience of Gratitude

Let's look at the science behind why gratitude works so powerfully.

When you practise gratitude consistently, your brain undergoes tangible, measurable changes. MRI scans show that gratitude:

- Activates the **ventromedial prefrontal cortex**, associated with reward, decision-making, and positive emotion

- Increases production of **dopamine and serotonin**, the "feel-good" neurotransmitters that elevate mood

- Strengthens the **neural pathways** linked to empathy, optimism, and resilience

In other words, gratitude rewires your brain for emotional stability, expanded awareness, and opportunity recognition.

One 2003 study by Dr Robert Emmons and Dr Michael McCullough found that people who kept a daily gratitude journal experienced:

- Higher levels of optimism

- More exercise and better sleep

- Increased motivation and fewer physical symptoms

Another study from the University of Pennsylvania found that a single act of writing a gratitude letter led to a significant increase in happiness levels, lasting up to a month.

Why? Because gratitude interrupts the brain's default survival mode. It shifts focus away from what's lacking to what's *working*, from threat to trust, from scarcity to *sufficiency*.

Gratitude doesn't mean you ignore reality.
It means you shift your relationship to it.

---

## How Gratitude Expands Your Abundance Perception

Scarcity shrinks your vision.
Gratitude *widens* it.

When you're focused on what you don't have, you become blind to what's right in front of you.
But when you practise gratitude, you retrain your attention. You start to notice:

- Kindness in strangers

- Opportunities in challenges

- Growth in discomfort

- Beauty in the ordinary

Suddenly, life feels *full*. Not perfect, not problem-free, but *rich* with possibility.

This expanded perception creates powerful outcomes:

- You feel more inspired to take positive action

- You become more magnetic to others (optimism is contagious)

- You make better decisions because you're operating from sufficiency, not desperation

This is how gratitude *accelerates* abundance.
 It puts you in the right frame of mind to recognise, receive, and respond to opportunity.

---

## Five Gratitude Practices That Shift Your Mindset Fast

Let's move from theory to action. Here are five practical gratitude tools you can start using today.

**1. The 3x3 Morning Ritual**

Every morning, write down:

- Three things you're grateful for

- Three things you're proud of

- Three things you're excited about

This combination activates gratitude, self-worth, and future vision, all key components of abundance thinking. It takes five minutes and sets your mindset for the day.

## 2. Gratitude Letter (But You Don't Have to Send It)

Write a heartfelt letter to someone who's impacted your life, past or present. Focus on what they gave you, how they helped you grow, and how you feel about it now.

Even if you never send it, the emotional clarity you gain is profound. And if you do send it? You'll often change someone else's life in the process.

## 3. Gratitude Walks

Take a 10-minute walk and speak your gratitude aloud (or silently, if you prefer). Thank your body, your environment, the people in your life, the lessons you've learned, even the challenges that shaped you.

This combines movement, nature, and presence, a triple win for rewiring your mindset.

## 4. Gratitude Jar

Keep a jar and slips of paper somewhere visible. Each day, write one thing you're grateful for and drop it in. Over time, this becomes a powerful visual reminder of your blessings. On tough days, read a few notes to realign.

## 5. Gratitude Reframing

When something frustrating happens, ask:

> "What's the gift here?"
> "What am I learning?"
> "What could this make possible?"

This doesn't mean toxic positivity. It means *choosing* to extract value from your experiences. Scarcity says: "This is awful." Gratitude says: "This might be preparing me."

---

## Real Story: How Gratitude Journaling Changed Leila's Life

Leila was in a rough spot. Recently divorced, in a job she didn't love, struggling with money and self-esteem. A friend gave her a journal and suggested writing three things she was grateful for each day.

At first, it felt pointless. She wrote things like, "I'm grateful I have toothpaste," or "I didn't cry today."

But she kept going. Slowly, her entries deepened:

- "I'm grateful I stood up for myself in that meeting."

- "I'm grateful for my daughter's laugh."

- "I'm grateful I had the courage to apply for a new role."

After three months, Leila's entire energy had shifted. She wasn't just *surviving* anymore, she was *seeing* herself differently. She landed a better job. Started dating again. Rebuilt her confidence.

When asked what changed, she said:

> "Nothing around me changed at first. But my mindset did. And then everything else followed."

---

## The Gratitude-Manifestation Link

Many people ask: *How does gratitude help me attract abundance?*

Here's how:
 Gratitude is the *emotional frequency* of abundance. When you're grateful, you feel *as if* you already have what you want. This aligns your brain with the experience of *having* rather than *lacking*.

When you feel rich internally, you start behaving like someone who expects good things. You show up differently. You make better choices. You take bigger steps. You become magnetic to opportunity.

Gratitude is not just a feel-good habit. It's a *practical strategy* for aligning with your most abundant self.

---

## Reflection: What Can You Appreciate Right Now?

Take five minutes. Write down your answers to the following:

1. What do I appreciate about myself today?

2. What's something small that brought me joy recently?

3. Who in my life am I especially grateful for right now?

4. What challenge has helped me grow?

5. What part of my life feels richer than I've acknowledged?

The more you practise this, the easier it becomes. And the easier it becomes, the more your brain begins to *default to abundance*.

## Takeaway

Gratitude isn't just a mindset tool. It's a *portal*.
 A portal to abundance, peace, creativity, clarity, joy.

It doesn't require perfect circumstances.
 It doesn't demand anything external.
 It's something you can practise anytime, anywhere.

And the best part?
 The more you do it, the more there is to be grateful for.

You don't have to wait for more to feel rich.
 You can *feel rich now*.
 And from that energy, everything changes.

# Chapter 9: The Power of Generosity

*"No one has ever become poor by giving." – Anne Frank*

---

## Giving Before You "Have Enough"

Let's start with a radical truth:

You don't give because you have abundance.
You create abundance *by giving*.

This is one of the great paradoxes of prosperity, and one that many people stuck in scarcity thinking struggle to accept. They believe they must first "make it," hoard, protect, and ensure they'll never run out before giving even a little.

But real abundance doesn't wait.
It acts as if more is already on the way.

And that's what generosity is:

> A mindset that trusts in flow, not finality.
> A statement that says, "There's enough, for me and for you."
> A choice to circulate energy, not just conserve it.

Generosity isn't about grand gestures or massive donations. It's not reserved for the rich.
 It's about how you show up, daily, consistently, with an open hand and heart.

Because giving, when done from alignment, doesn't deplete you.
 It *expands* you.

---

## Why Giving Is Essential to Abundance

Let's unpack why generosity is so potent as an abundance accelerator.

### 1. Giving Rewires Scarcity at Its Core

Scarcity says: "Hold onto what you have. There may not be more."
 Generosity says: "I trust that what I give returns to me in some form."

Every time you give freely, your time, your help, your attention, your money, you're sending a message to your subconscious: *I have enough.*

That belief rewires your brain to see the world through a lens of sufficiency. And when you live in that state, opportunities and connections begin to flow back to you.

### 2. Giving Puts You in the Creator Role

Scarcity makes you reactive. You wait. You withhold. You play defence.

But giving makes you proactive. It says, *"I create value. I am a contributor."*

This shift from taker to *giver* is one of the most profound mindset flips in personal growth. You stop thinking like a consumer of life, and start thinking like a *source* of possibility.

### 3. Giving Builds Connection, Trust, and Influence

Whether you're in business, leadership, or simply human relationships, generosity builds trust. It signals confidence. People are drawn to those who give without keeping score.

Over time, your reputation becomes an asset. And that often leads to referrals, collaborations, support, loyalty, forms of wealth that compound over time.

---

## Generosity Beyond Money

Too often, we limit the idea of generosity to financial giving. But abundance shows up in many forms:

- **Time**: Listening deeply, mentoring someone, helping a neighbour

- **Skills**: Sharing your knowledge freely, offering advice, supporting a cause

- **Energy**: Celebrating others, sending thoughtful messages, encouraging someone privately

- **Presence**: Truly *being with* someone, without distraction, judgement, or rush

- **Kindness**: Smiling, forgiving, making someone's day lighter

Sometimes, the most generous thing you can do is *see* someone fully and remind them of their worth.

That's abundance in action.

---

## Overcoming the Fear: "But I Don't Have Enough to Give"

This is where many people get stuck.
They think: *"I barely have enough for myself, how can I give anything away?"*

Here's the mindset shift:

> Generosity isn't about giving from *excess*,
> it's about giving from *belief*.

You don't give because you've reached some imaginary threshold of "having enough."
You give because you believe that giving *doesn't diminish you*, it expands you.

Start small. Start sincere.

- Buy someone a coffee.

- Share a helpful post or article.

- Offer a testimonial for a product or service you love.

- Send a voice note to someone going through a tough time.

- Give a genuine compliment.

These tiny acts create ripple effects. Not just in the world, but in your own heart and mind.

They affirm: *I am not empty. I have something to give.*

And in time, you'll find that what you gave returns in ways you never expected.

---

## Case Study: Giving Without Waiting

## Meet Ravi – The Generous Start-Up Founder

Ravi was building a freelance design business. He was still early in his journey, barely making ends meet. But he made a decision early on: he would *always* give, even when it felt inconvenient.

Every Friday, he offered a free one-hour design audit for small business owners who couldn't afford his full services. He'd share actionable feedback, ideas, and encouragement, no strings attached.

His friends thought he was mad. "Shouldn't you be chasing paying clients instead?"

But Ravi trusted in value-first generosity.

Over time, those business owners referred him to paying clients. One of them became his biggest long-term contract. Another connected him with an investor who later funded his agency. That Friday hour built a reputation that money couldn't buy.

Today, Ravi runs a thriving six-figure business. He still offers free audits. But now, they're booked out three months in advance.

When asked what made the difference, he said:

> "I didn't wait until I was rich to act like I had something to give. That's what made me rich."

## Generosity as a Lifestyle, Not a Moment

Abundant people don't treat giving as a duty.
They treat it as an *identity*.

It's not just something they do, it's who they are.

They look for ways to uplift, add value, surprise,
appreciate. Not because they expect something in
return, but because they trust that generosity creates a
life rich with meaning, connection, and flow.

And here's the secret:

> The most generous people are often the
> most joyful.
> And the most joyful people are often the
> most magnetic.
> And the most magnetic people attract the
> most opportunity.

See the pattern?

## Reflection: Expanding Your Generosity Identity

Take a few minutes to reflect:

1. Where in my life am I already generous, but haven't given myself credit for it?

2. What form of generosity feels easiest or most natural to me, time, energy, encouragement, service?

3. What's one small way I could give today, from alignment not obligation?

4. What belief do I need to adopt to become someone who gives freely and confidently?

Write your answers down. Let generosity become a *practice*, not a performance.

---

## Takeaway

You don't need more money to start being generous.
 You need more *trust*.

Trust that what you give comes back.
 Trust that you are a source, not a vessel.
 Trust that abundance isn't something you hold, it's something you *circulate*.

Generosity is not the reward for abundance.
 It's the *route* to it.

So ask yourself:

> Who can I help today?
>  Where can I give from love, not fear?

Then act.

Because every time you give, you send a message to life:

> "I believe in plenty."

And life responds in kind.

# Chapter 10: Expanding Your Circle of Influence

*"You are the average of the five people you spend the most time with." – Jim Rohn*

---

## Your Environment Is More Powerful Than You Think

It's been said that mindset is everything. But here's the less talked about truth:

### Your mindset is shaped by your environment.

You can read every book, repeat affirmations, practise gratitude, but if you're surrounded by scarcity thinking, it will seep into you.

We absorb beliefs like we absorb accents: subtly, consistently, unconsciously.

Spend time with people who complain, play small, and fear change?
You'll eventually do the same.

Spend time with people who talk ideas, build things, and stretch themselves?

You'll start to think bigger, take more risks, and trust your potential.

That's why upgrading your circle of influence is one of the *fastest ways* to shift into an abundance mindset.

You don't just become what you believe.
You become what your *environment* believes.

---

## Scarcity and Abundance Are Contagious

Think of scarcity and abundance like emotional viruses, they're both contagious.

Scarcity infects through:

- Gossip and criticism

- Fear-based decision-making

- Jealousy masked as concern

- Subtle sabotage ("Don't get your hopes up")

- Normalising stress, struggle, and self-sacrifice

Abundance spreads through:

- Encouragement and possibility

- Celebrating wins without envy

- Solution-focused conversations

- High standards and belief in others

- Openness to collaboration and growth

The people around you are either reinforcing your limitations or expanding your potential. There's rarely a neutral.

And here's the kicker:

> Even one negative voice can drown out your inner abundance.
> That's why your circle matters *so much*.

---

## You Don't Need to Cut People Off, But You *Do* Need to Be Conscious

Now, this isn't about ghosting your friends or family. It's not about superiority or judgement. It's about *strategy*.

There are people in your life you love deeply, but who live in scarcity. Maybe they fear risk. Maybe they don't understand your dreams. Maybe they mean well but constantly plant doubt.

You don't have to abandon them. But you *must* counterbalance them with others who stretch and inspire you.

Think of your relationships like meals. You can handle a few indulgences, but your *main diet* must be nourishing. Your emotional and mental circle should feed your growth, not your fear.

---

## How to Curate an Abundant Circle

Let's get practical. Here's how to start shaping a circle that reflects your future, not your past.

### 1. Audit Your Current Circle

Ask yourself:

- Who uplifts me?

- Who drains me?

- Who challenges me to grow?

- Who enables my limitations?

- Who celebrates my wins without jealousy?

- Who helps me believe in what's possible?

Write down names. Be honest. This audit isn't about guilt, it's about *awareness*.

## 2. Seek Out Abundance-Minded Communities

Where do people who think big hang out? Where do dreamers, builders, creators, givers gather?

Look for:

- Masterminds and group coaching programmes

- Coworking spaces or entrepreneur meetups

- Personal development conferences

- Local networking events

- Online communities focused on growth

Proximity matters, even virtually. The goal is to get in rooms (physical or digital) where expansion is the norm.

## 3. Follow Thought Leaders Who Challenge You

Who are your digital mentors? Who fills your feed?

Unfollow the noise. Follow the *builders*. Fill your mind with podcasts, books, and content that reinforce abundance, courage, and possibility.

Let their energy lift your standards until yours match theirs.

### 4. Invest in Mentorship or Coaching

Want to fast-track your growth? Hire someone who lives in the mindset you're building. You're not just paying for knowledge, you're paying for *exposure to belief*.

Being in the energy of someone who's five steps ahead of you can collapse years of trial and error.

You'll rise simply by being around their confidence, clarity, and standards.

---

# Case Study: From Playing Small to Thinking Big

### Meet Jordan – The Quiet Freelancer with Big Potential

Jordan was a talented copywriter with a handful of clients and a steady, modest income. But he couldn't seem to break past a certain threshold. Every time he tried to raise his rates or pitch bigger clients, something held him back.

He was part of a group chat with other freelancers who constantly complained about "bad clients," "dead markets," and "low-ball offers." He realised: *I've normalised struggle as the standard.*

Jordan joined a mastermind of high-level creative entrepreneurs. The conversations were different, strategic, empowered, abundant. People shared wins, gave referrals, offered insights. No one complained about rates, they set them unapologetically.

Within six months, Jordan doubled his income. But more than that, he started showing up differently, bolder, clearer, more confident.

When asked what changed, he said:

> "I upgraded my circle. And that upgraded my belief in what was possible for me."

---

## You Don't Need to Be the Smartest in the Room

In fact, you *shouldn't* be.

If you're the most driven, optimistic, growth-focused person in your circle, you're in the wrong room.

Find circles where:

- You feel a little uncomfortable (in the best way)

- People are already living the life you aspire to

- You're not the expert, you're the *student*

- The norm is excellence, not mediocrity

Your next level is rarely a solo project.
It's almost always a *collaboration of influence*.

---

## Reflection: Who's Shaping Your Mindset?

Take 10 minutes and answer these:

1. Who are the five people I spend the most time with?

2. How do each of them impact my energy, mindset, and choices?

3. Who in my life reflects the mindset I want to embody?

4. What's one step I can take this week to spend more time in an abundant environment?

You don't have to overhaul your life overnight.
Start with one conversation. One new connection. One upgrade.

---

## Takeaway

Abundance isn't just what you *think*.
It's what you *absorb* from the people around you.

If you want to grow, you need to be in the presence of people who already believe what you're trying to believe.

Because success doesn't happen in isolation.
It happens in community.

So step into the rooms where abundance is spoken fluently.
Where dreaming big isn't strange, it's expected.
Where celebrating success isn't arrogance, it's *inspiration*.

And watch what happens when your circle expands, your life will, too.

# Chapter 11: Saying Yes to Opportunities

*"If someone offers you an amazing opportunity and you're not sure you can do it, say yes, then learn how to do it later." – Richard Branson*

---

## When Scarcity Says "No" to Your Future

Opportunities often knock quietly.

They don't always look like golden tickets. Sometimes they arrive as awkward emails, strange coincidences, or unexpected introductions. And most people miss them, not because they're invisible, but because they're afraid.

> Scarcity says: "What if I fail?"
> Abundance says: "What if this changes everything?"

Your mindset determines how you respond to chance. Scarcity will train you to say no, out of fear, perfectionism, imposter syndrome, or a belief that you're not ready. It'll have you waiting for perfect timing, perfect confidence, perfect conditions.

But perfection is a myth. And waiting often means missing.

Abundance, on the other hand, is a *yes* mindset. It doesn't say yes to everything blindly. But it says yes to possibility. It says yes to *becoming*. It says yes before you're fully ready, because that's how you *get* ready.

---

## How Scarcity Keeps You Saying No

Let's examine the real reasons people say no to opportunities:

### 1. Fear of Failure

"If I try and it doesn't work, I'll look foolish. I'll waste time. I'll lose money."

This fear isn't irrational, it's learned. You may have grown up seeing failure as shameful, not useful. But the truth is: *failure is feedback*. Every successful person has said yes before knowing they'd succeed.

### 2. Fear of Rejection

"What if I apply and they say no? What if I pitch and get ignored?"

Scarcity convinces you that rejection is proof of inadequacy. Abundance reframes rejection as *redirection*. A "no" doesn't close the door, it moves you closer to the right one.

### 3. Imposter Syndrome

"Who am I to go for that? I'm not qualified. I'm not experienced enough."

Scarcity tells you to wait until you're *certified* by someone else. Abundance reminds you that most successful people built competence *after* they started, not before.

### 4. Perfection Paralysis

"If I can't do it perfectly, I won't do it at all."

This is a control mechanism rooted in fear. But growth lives in imperfection. Abundant thinkers start messy, adjust quickly, and trust the process.

---

## Abundance Thinkers Look for Reasons to Say Yes

Opportunity rarely comes gift-wrapped with a guarantee. It usually comes disguised as:

- A stretch assignment at work

- An invitation to speak, write, or collaborate

- A new idea that feels scary but exciting

- A chance to invest, launch, or lead before you feel "qualified"

- A connection that could change everything, if you follow up

Abundant thinkers don't let doubt drive the decision. They assess risk, yes, but they also weigh *potential*.

They ask:

> "What's the worst that could happen?"
> "What's the best that could happen?"
> "What would the future version of me do?"

And most importantly: *"What could I miss out on by saying no?"*

---

## Saying Yes Doesn't Mean Saying Yes to Everything

Let's be clear: abundance doesn't mean saying yes indiscriminately. It means:

- Saying yes to aligned opportunities

- Saying yes to growth, even when it's uncomfortable

- Saying yes to things that stretch, not stress you

- Saying yes to new versions of yourself, even if they scare you

It's about discernment, not desperation. You're not chasing. You're *responding to life* with openness and courage.

---

## Story: The Pivotal "Yes" That Changed Everything

### Meet Amina – The Reluctant Public Speaker

Amina was a brilliant wellness coach with a loyal client base. Soft-spoken and humble, she preferred behind-the-scenes work. Then came the email:

A popular wellness podcast wanted to interview her. Her first thought? *"Absolutely not. I'm not ready. What if I mess up?"*

She almost deleted it. But something in her whispered: *"Say yes. Stretch. This is bigger than you."*

She accepted, nervously. She prepared obsessively. Her hands trembled during the interview, but she showed up. She told her story with honesty and heart.

That episode went viral. It brought hundreds of new clients, speaking invitations, book interest, and a level of visibility she never imagined.

When asked about the moment she hit "reply," she said:

> "That one yes cracked my whole life open. I wasn't ready. I just decided to say yes anyway."

---

## Spotting Opportunities You've Been Ignoring

Sometimes, the opportunity is already in your inbox. Or your DMs. Or your mind.

Here's how to spot the chances that scarcity might be making you overlook:

- What have I *almost* said yes to but pulled back from?

- What do I secretly want to do but tell myself I'm not ready for?

- What invitations, ideas, or connections have I downplayed out of fear?

- What would I say yes to if I fully believed in myself?

Your answers will point to opportunities already orbiting your life.

And remember: it's not just about *huge* moments. Sometimes, saying yes to a walk, a workshop, or a warm intro leads to a life-changing chain reaction.

---

## Managing the Fear That Comes With Saying Yes

Saying yes often brings a companion: fear. That's normal. Fear doesn't mean stop. It means *you're moving*.

Here's how to manage it:

### 1. Name It

Say it aloud: "I'm scared of failing. I'm scared of looking silly. I'm scared of being seen."

Naming the fear disarms it. Hiding it gives it power.

### 2. Anchor in Identity

Ask: "What would the abundant version of me do?" Let that version decide, not the scared one.

### 3. Use the 10-10-10 Rule

How will I feel about this decision in:

- 10 minutes?

- 10 months?

- 10 years?

This zooms you out from temporary fear to long-term vision.

### 4. Act Before You Overthink

Courage isn't the absence of fear, it's action *with* fear. Often, the longer you wait, the louder doubt becomes. Decide fast, then figure it out as you go.

---

## Reflection: What Yes Is Waiting for You?

Take a moment and write:

1. What's one opportunity I've been hesitating to say yes to?

2. What's the real fear behind my hesitation?

3. What might happen if I said yes anyway?

4. What would I gain, even if it didn't work out perfectly?

Then decide: will you move forward *despite* the fear?

---

## Takeaway

Saying yes isn't just about seizing opportunities.
 It's about affirming belief in yourself.

It's saying:

> *"I trust myself to rise."*
> *"I'm ready for more."*
> *"I don't have to be perfect, I just have to begin."*

Because life doesn't wait for you to feel ready.
 It rewards those who are *willing*.

So the next time a door opens, and fear whispers "maybe later," pause.
 And choose the path of abundance.

Say yes.

Even before you're ready.

# Chapter 12: Mastering Abundant Decision-Making

*"In every single thing you do, you are choosing a direction. Your life is a product of choices." – Dr Kathleen Hall*

---

## The Hidden Mindset Behind Every Choice

Take a look at your life right now, your income, your relationships, your career, your health.

All of it has been shaped by one thing: **your decisions**.

Not just the big ones, like what job to take or where to live, but the small, daily choices:

- Do I invest in myself or play it safe?

- Do I reach out or stay silent?

- Do I take the leap or stay where I'm comfortable?

Now here's the key question:

Are your decisions rooted in *abundance* or *scarcity*?

Because every choice you make, whether it's how you spend your time, what you say yes to, or how you respond to a challenge, is a *vote*. A vote for growth or stagnation. Expansion or contraction. Possibility or limitation.

You can't live abundantly with scarcity-coded decision-making.

It's time to bring clarity and confidence back into your choices, and start making decisions like someone who believes in their future.

---

## How Scarcity Clouds Decision-Making

Scarcity creates cognitive fog. It puts your brain in survival mode, making it difficult to access creativity, logic, or vision. It shrinks your thinking to what's urgent, not what's *important*.

Here's how it commonly shows up:

### 1. Fear-Based Hesitation

You delay action until conditions are "perfect." This leads to missed opportunities, eroded confidence, and slow progress.

### 2. Short-Term Thinking

You focus on immediate costs rather than long-term gains. You avoid investments in favour of savings, even when that choice slows your growth.

### 3. Overanalysing and Paralysis

You overthink every possible outcome, obsess over failure, and talk yourself out of action. The result? Stagnation disguised as "being cautious."

### 4. Avoiding Risk Entirely

You say no to change, even when the status quo is unsatisfying. You stick to what's familiar, not because it's working, but because it's *known*.

These are not logical decisions. They're *protective*. But protection becomes a prison when it blocks your potential.

---

## What Abundant Decision-Making Looks Like

Abundance-minded people don't make perfect decisions, they make *progressive* ones. They choose with courage, alignment, and long-term vision in mind.

Abundant decision-making is:

- Rooted in *possibility*, not panic

- Driven by *vision*, not immediate validation

- Guided by *growth*, not guilt

- Focused on *what could go right*, not just what could go wrong

They understand this core truth:

> **Every decision teaches you something, either how to succeed or how to improve.**

With that mindset, no choice is wasted.

---

## The Power of Long-Term Thinking

Scarcity focuses on now:

- "Can I afford this today?"

- "What if I fail this week?"

- "What do people think right now?"

Abundance zooms out:

- "How will this impact me next year?"

- "What if this sets up something bigger?"

- "What does future me thank me for?"

This long-term lens doesn't ignore the present. But it uses the *future* to inform today's action.

**Ask yourself:**

- If I make this decision consistently for the next 12 months, where will it take me?

- Will this help me become the person I'm trying to be?

- Am I choosing comfort over expansion?

Sometimes, the best decision feels uncomfortable in the short term, but leads to massive rewards in the long run.

---

## Investment Thinking vs Cost Thinking

This mindset shift is a game-changer.

People with a scarcity mindset view everything as a **cost**.
 They ask: *"What will this take from me?"*

People with an abundance mindset see many things as an **investment**.
 They ask: *"What could this create for me?"*

Let's break it down:

| Scenario | Cost Thinking | Investment Thinking |
|---|---|---|
| Paying for a course | "Too expensive" | "This could increase my earning power" |
| Hiring a coach | "I can't justify it" | "This could accelerate my growth" |
| Delegating tasks | "I'll lose money" | "This frees me to focus on higher value" |
| Going on a retreat | "That's indulgent" | "This could reset my mindset and vision" |

The key difference?
 Cost thinkers focus on *what they lose*.
 Investment thinkers focus on *what they gain*.

That one shift changes *everything*.

# Case Study: Two Business Owners, Two Mindsets

### *Sophie – The Cautious Creative*

Sophie ran a successful online shop. She had decent traffic, loyal customers, and solid reviews. When she was offered a chance to license her products through a national retailer, she hesitated.

Why? Because she was worried about scaling too fast, losing control, and potentially disappointing new buyers.

She turned the offer down.

Six months later, a competitor took the same deal, and quadrupled their revenue. Sophie stayed safe. But she stayed *small*.

Her decision was based on fear. And fear, while understandable, kept her stuck.

### *Daniel – The Abundant Strategist*

Daniel was a freelance developer. When offered a contract to build software for a startup in exchange for equity, he paused. He needed money, not shares.

But he zoomed out. He researched the company. He believed in their mission. He negotiated a partial payment and partial equity.

Three years later, the startup sold. Daniel's equity was worth more than his *previous five years of income combined*.

He made a decision that didn't pay off instantly, but changed his life long term.

That's investment thinking. That's abundant strategy.

---

## Your Decision-Making Upgrade Toolkit

Ready to make better, braver decisions? Use these tools:

### 1. The 24-Hour Rule

Don't make major decisions in a state of fear, frustration, or fatigue. Wait, reflect, and revisit with a clearer mind.

### 2. Reverse Engineer from the Future

Ask: "If I were already living my abundant life, what would I choose right now?" Let that version of you lead.

### 3. List Costs vs Consequences

What is the cost of taking action?
What is the consequence of *not* taking action?

Sometimes, the price of staying the same is higher than the risk of change.

## 4. Name the Emotion Behind the Resistance

Is it fear? Guilt? Imposter syndrome? Scarcity?
Once you name the emotion, you can separate it from the *logic* of the decision.

---

## Reflection: Aligning with Abundant Choices

Write your answers to the following:

1. What's a decision I've been putting off because of fear?

2. What might my future self say about this choice?

3. Am I focusing on cost, or on potential return?

4. What would an abundant version of me do right now?

These answers will bring clarity, and courage.

---

## Takeaway

Every day, you cast votes with your choices.
And over time, those votes create your reality.

Are you voting for safety or expansion?
Are you acting from fear or from faith?
Are you choosing what's familiar, or what aligns with who you want to become?

Mastering abundant decision-making doesn't mean being perfect.
It means being *aligned*.
And being willing to choose growth, even when it feels uncertain.

Because the best decisions?
They rarely feel "safe."
But they always lead somewhere *greater*.

# Chapter 13: Developing Multiple Streams of Income

*"Never depend on a single income. Make investment to create a second source." – Warren Buffett*

---

## Dependency Is a Scarcity Strategy

If all your income comes from one source, whether it's a job, a single client, or one product, you're not in control. You're vulnerable.

Scarcity tells you to keep things simple. Stick with what you know. Be grateful for that one paycheck.

But abundance says: *"There's more where that came from, and I can build it."*

Abundance isn't just about having more, it's about creating *multiple pathways* for wealth, freedom, and flow.

The truth is: most millionaires don't earn their wealth from one stream. They cultivate several. Some are active. Some are passive. But they all contribute to a life that isn't dependent on a single economic pillar.

Why? Because **diversification is freedom**.

When you have multiple income streams, you're no longer tied to the fate of one employer, one client, or one industry. You can navigate change, take time off, or pivot without panic.

You're in charge.

---

## Scarcity Keeps You in "One Channel" Thinking

Scarcity thinking often creates the following false beliefs:

- "I don't have time to earn money in other ways."

- "I'm not business-minded."

- "Passive income is for influencers or tech wizards."

- "I can't monetise my skills, I don't have anything valuable to offer."

- "It's too risky to branch out."

These beliefs are convenient for staying in your comfort zone. But they're not *true*. They're just *unpractised*.

And the longer you believe them, the longer you stay reliant on just one stream, no matter how strong that stream may seem.

---

## Abundance Thinkers Ask: "What Else Is Possible?"

When you adopt an abundance mindset, you begin to see income not just as survival, but as *creative expression*.

You ask different questions:

- "What skills do I already have that could serve others?"

- "How can I create value that continues to pay me over time?"

- "What's something I could build once and earn from repeatedly?"

- "What if money could flow to me from multiple places, even while I sleep?"

That's the shift. From income as labour… to income as *leverage*.

## Practical Strategies for Creating Additional Income Streams

You don't need to quit your job or become a serial entrepreneur to diversify your income. You just need to start where you are, with what you have.

Here are several categories to explore:

## 1. Side Hustles

Active income streams you build in your spare time.

Examples:

- Freelancing (design, writing, consulting, virtual assistance)

- Teaching or tutoring online

- Selling handmade products

- Dog walking, babysitting, or local services

- Driving for delivery or ride-share platforms

- Event photography or mobile car valeting

☐ **Tip**: Pick something that leverages skills you already have. Don't start from scratch, start from *strength*.

---

## 2. Digital Products

Create once, sell repeatedly.

Examples:

- E-books or self-published guides

- Online courses or workshops

- Templates, planners, or design kits

- Print-on-demand merchandise

- Membership sites or exclusive communities

☐ **Tip**: Focus on solving one clear problem. Simplicity sells.

---

## 3. Service-Based Income Expansion

Offer new packages or pivot how you deliver.

Examples:

- Add premium tiers to existing services

- Offer retainer models or subscription plans

- Create a "done-for-you" or group version of your one-to-one work

 

⬜ **Tip**: Repackage what's already working at a higher value or lower maintenance.

---

## 4. Passive Income and Investments

Money that works for you after the initial setup.

Examples:

- Dividend stocks or ETFs

- Property rental (short-term or long-term)

- Peer-to-peer lending

- Royalties from books, music, or licensing

- Affiliate marketing (recommending products and earning a commission)

☐ **Tip**: Start small. Even a £100 monthly return from an investment is a *stream*, and streams grow.

---

## 5. Skill Monetisation

Turn hobbies, talents, or experience into income.

Examples:

- Sell art, crafts, or photography

- Launch a blog or YouTube channel around a niche

- Offer coaching, mentoring, or life advice based on personal experience

- Host local workshops or virtual training sessions

☐ **Tip**: Think: "What do people already ask me for help with?" That's your monetisable gift.

---

## Story: Three Ordinary People, Three Streams of Change

### Case 1: Hannah – The Office Admin Turned Etsy Seller

Hannah worked full-time in admin, with little savings and big dreams. She loved calligraphy, so she started creating hand-lettered wedding signage in the evenings. She opened an Etsy store with just five listings.

Within a year, it was bringing in £1,200 a month, more than her car payment and food budget combined. It became her bridge to part-time work and eventually full-time entrepreneurship.

### Case 2: Liam – The Secondary Teacher Turned Property Investor

Liam saved aggressively for two years and used a help-to-buy scheme to purchase a small flat. He rented out a room and reinvested the income into a second property. Over seven years, he built a portfolio of five rentals.

Now, his teaching salary is optional. His passive rental income covers all essentials, and then some.

### Case 3: Sarah – The Nurse Who Wrote a Digital Guide

Sarah, a registered nurse, created a downloadable PDF titled *"The New Mum's Hospital Checklist"*, packed with preparation tips from her professional experience. She priced it at £12.99.

With zero tech background, she made £5,000 in her first three months. Why? Because she solved a *specific* problem with a unique insight. And it became a true income stream, built once, sold repeatedly.

---

## Your Streams Don't Need to Be Big, They Need to Be *Built*

You don't need to earn six figures from a new stream for it to matter.

- £250 a month from a side hustle? That's £3,000 a year.

- £80 a week from passive income? That's a new holiday paid for.

- £500 from selling an online course? That's momentum, and proof.

The key isn't scale, it's *stacking*.

One stream. Then another. Then another. Until you're no longer dependent… you're *diversified*.

---

## Reflection: Where Could You Start?

Ask yourself:

1. What skills, interests, or experiences do I already have that others value?

2. What problems could I solve quickly with a guide, tool, or service?

3. What have I said "I should try that" about, but never pursued?

4. What's one simple step I can take this week to test an idea?

Start with curiosity. Don't chase perfection. Build momentum.

---

## Takeaway

Scarcity says: *"Stick to what you know. Don't spread yourself too thin."*
 Abundance says: *"You're capable of creating more. Don't let comfort become a cage."*

Multiple income streams aren't about greed. They're about *freedom*.

Freedom to walk away.
 Freedom to build on your terms.
 Freedom to sleep at night knowing you have *options*.

And the best time to start?
 Now.
 Not when you "have more time." Not when you "feel
ready."

The seed of abundance is in your hands.
 Plant it. Water it. Let it grow.

# Chapter 14: Healing Scarcity in Relationships

*"You can have everything in life you want, if you will just help enough other people get what they want." – Zig Ziglar*

---

## Scarcity Doesn't Just Live in Your Wallet, It Lives in Your Relationships

When we talk about scarcity, most people think of money. But scarcity thinking doesn't stop at finances, it shows up in how we *connect* with others.

If you believe there's "not enough" in the world, not enough love, success, validation, energy, you'll start to compete, compare, and close off.

You might:

- Keep score in your marriage.

- Feel jealous when friends succeed.

- Withhold praise, affection, or credit.

- Fear abandonment or betrayal, even without cause.

- Struggle to trust others fully.

- Say "yes" when you mean "no" to avoid rejection.

All of this stems from one underlying belief:

> *"If someone else gets more… I'll end up with less."*

But that's not how abundance works.
 Love isn't pie. Kindness doesn't run out. Connection isn't a competition.

Abundance in relationships means **believing there's enough to go around, and acting like it.**

---

## How Scarcity Sabotages Connection

Let's look at the subtle ways scarcity can erode our most important relationships:

### 1. Jealousy and Comparison

You scroll through social media and see a friend's holiday, job promotion, or happy relationship, and instead of celebrating, you shrink. You start to think you're behind. That you're not doing enough. That there's not enough success left for you.

Scarcity turns someone else's win into your personal loss.

### 2. Withholding and Self-Protecting

You're afraid to be vulnerable. You keep emotions bottled up. You don't ask for help. You hide your true needs because you fear being a burden, or worse, being rejected.

Scarcity whispers: *"If I open up, I'll be hurt."*

### 3. Control and Competition

You try to "win" arguments. You interrupt to prove your point. You keep emotional tabs or expect others to "earn" your love and attention.

Scarcity says: *"If I'm not in control, I'll be taken advantage of."*

### 4. Over-Giving to Earn Worth

Ironically, scarcity can also show up as *over-functioning*, doing everything for everyone, hoping to earn approval, affection, or inclusion.

Abundance doesn't mean being everything to everyone. It means knowing you're enough even when you're *not everything*.

---

## What Abundance in Relationships Looks Like

Let's shift gears. What does an abundant relationship mindset look like?

It's not perfect harmony 24/7. It's not boundless positivity. It's grounded, generous, and growth-focused.

Abundance in relationships means:

- **Celebrating others without shrinking yourself**

- **Communicating openly without fear of rejection**

- **Trusting that love, time, energy, and joy are renewable**

- **Supporting others without expecting immediate return**

- **Seeing others as partners, not threats**

It's built on collaboration, not competition. On contribution, not keeping score.

---

## A Story of Transformation: From Scorekeeping to Synergy

### Meet Ella and James

Ella and James had been married for eight years. They were solid on paper: two kids, decent income, a shared home. But their emotional connection had grown cold.

Fights often revolved around who did more:
Ella felt unseen for the invisible labour she did at home.
James felt underappreciated for working long hours.
Neither felt like they were "winning", and both were exhausted.

When they attended a couples' coaching weekend, one concept changed everything: **abundance over accounting**.

They realised they'd turned their marriage into a ledger. Every act of service, every missed moment, every forgotten gesture was tallied and mentally filed.

But connection isn't built on maths. It's built on meaning.

They began shifting:

- From *"What have you done for me?"* to *"How can I support you?"*

- From *"I need to protect my energy"* to *"Let's create energy together"*

- From *"There's only so much love/time/attention"* to *"We can create more by giving freely"*

The change didn't happen overnight. But slowly, the tension eased. The laughter returned. And they stopped fighting to win, and started fighting for *each other*.

---

## Building Abundant Relationships: Practical Shifts

Here's how to infuse your connections, romantic, platonic, familial, with abundance:

### 1. Celebrate Loudly and Often

When someone you love wins, celebrate like it's your own victory. Make it normal to say, "I'm so proud of you," "You inspire me," or "That's incredible."

Let celebration replace comparison.

### 2. Assume the Best

Instead of assuming others are out to get you, forget you, or neglect you, assume positive intent.

Abundance assumes *trust first*. Scarcity assumes *doubt first*.

### 3. Give Without Expecting Immediate Return

Offer support, kindness, praise, and presence without mentally tallying the score. Be the giver. Abundance flows through generosity, not barter.

### 4. Ask for What You Need Without Guilt

Scarcity says, "Don't ask, they'll think you're too much." Abundance says, "Your needs matter, and so do theirs."

Expressing needs is a gift of intimacy, not a burden.

### 5. Use "We" Language

Shifting from "me vs you" to "us together" can change the tone of your interactions.

Instead of "You never help around the house," try "How can we make this feel more balanced?"

Abundance speaks from partnership, not blame.

---

## The Community Effect: Scarcity vs Abundance in Groups

This mindset shift isn't just for couples, it applies to friendships, teams, and communities.

Scarcity in groups sounds like:

- Gossip

- Gatekeeping

- Cliques

- Competition over collaboration

- Hoarding knowledge or credit

Abundance in groups sounds like:

- Sharing freely

- Supporting others' wins

- Introducing people to opportunities

- Offering help before it's asked for

- Building something *together*

If you want to create an abundant life, surround yourself with people who are building one, too.

---

## Reflection: Your Relationship Mindset

1. In what relationships do I notice myself shrinking, withholding, or competing?

2. What's the fear underneath that behaviour?

3. What's one thing I can say or do this week to shift that relationship toward abundance?

4. Who in my life models abundant, generous love, and how can I learn from them?

---

## Takeaway

You were never meant to thrive alone.
 Abundance was designed to flow *through* connection, not around it.

When you stop competing and start collaborating, you unlock more than just love, you unlock power.

Power to build.
 Power to heal.
 Power to receive *and* to give.

Because there is enough love. Enough support. Enough space for everyone to win.

And when you bring abundance into your relationships, you don't just change how you connect, you change what's possible *together*.

# Chapter 15: Abundance in Career & Business

*"Don't be afraid to give up the good to go for the great."*
*– John D. Rockefeller*

---

## How Big Are You Willing to Think?

There's a quote often attributed to Michelangelo:

> *"The greater danger for most of us is not that our aim is too high and we miss it, but that it is too low and we reach it."*

Scarcity thinking doesn't just limit your bank balance, it limits your **vision**. It keeps your career "realistic." It whispers:

- "Just keep your head down and stay employed."

- "Don't draw too much attention to yourself."

- "They won't hire you, you don't tick all the boxes."

- "You're not qualified to charge that."

- "Now's not the time to grow, it's too risky."

And before you know it, you've been working within an invisible box. Safe. Steady. Small.

But abundance doesn't work in boxes. It works in *possibility*.

Abundant professionals don't just ask:

> *"What role can I get?"*
> They ask:
> *"What value can I create?"*

They don't just climb the ladder, they build new ones. They don't just work harder, they work **braver**.

This chapter is about stepping into that mindset. Because the biggest breakthroughs don't happen in your comfort zone. They happen when you start thinking *bigger*, about who you are, what you're capable of, and what kind of career or business you deserve.

---

## The Career-Limiting Power of Scarcity

Let's name some common scarcity-driven behaviours in professional life:

### 1. Staying in Roles You've Outgrown

Because it's "secure." Or because you're afraid to start again.

But staying safe is not the same as staying fulfilled.

### 2. Undercharging or Underselling Yourself

You worry about what people can afford or whether you're "worth it."

Scarcity equates self-worth with modesty. Abundance aligns it with *value*.

### 3. Hiding Your Work

You create but don't promote. You network, but you never ask. You fear being seen.

But visibility isn't arrogance, it's *accessibility*.

### 4. Viewing Others as Competition

You see other people's success as a threat. You feel envious, anxious, or resentful.

But competition is only threatening if you don't trust in your own unique value.

---

## The Abundant Way to Build a Career or Business

So how do abundant thinkers approach work differently?

They expand. They share. They collaborate. They play long games. And they keep showing up, especially when things feel uncertain.

Here's what that looks like in action:

---

## 1. Thinking Beyond the Job Description

Scarcity says, "Stick to your role."
Abundance says, "Solve the problem, then create new roles."

Abundant professionals spot gaps, offer new ideas, and initiate change. They don't wait to be told what to do, they *lead*.

Ask yourself:

- Where am I waiting for permission that I could be taking initiative?

- What strengths am I not using in my current role?

- What projects or problems light me up?

When you operate from abundance, your value becomes obvious, and opportunities start finding *you*.

## 2. Collaborating Instead of Competing

Abundance-minded professionals don't gatekeep. They share contacts. They recommend others. They refer work, even to "competitors."

Why? Because they know there's **more than enough**.

Collaboration is the fastest way to accelerate your growth, personally and professionally.

> "If you want to go fast, go alone. If you want to go far, go together." – African Proverb

Start asking:

- Who do I admire in my industry?

- What could we build or do *together*?

- Who can I lift up or open doors for?

## 3. Becoming Boldly Visible

Abundance understands that visibility = opportunity. People can't hire, promote, refer, or collaborate with you if they don't know you exist.

This doesn't mean becoming a self-promoter. It means being *strategically vocal* about the value you bring.

Post your wins. Share insights. Let people know what you're working on.

Visibility leads to trust. Trust leads to opportunity.

And opportunity? That's the *currency* of abundance.

---

## 4. Taking Brave Leaps Before You Feel Ready

Abundant people *apply* for the role they don't feel 100% qualified for.
 They *pitch* the client that seems out of reach.
 They *launch* the product before it's perfect.

They don't wait until they feel "enough." They trust they'll *grow into it*.

That leap creates momentum. And momentum magnetises opportunity.

---

## Story: Thinking Big Pays Off – The Case of Maria

Maria was a mid-level marketing manager at a large tech firm. She was competent, hardworking, and... invisible.

She did excellent work, but rarely spoke up in meetings. She didn't network. She avoided self-promotion. Her goal? "Keep my head down and not make mistakes."

Then came a company-wide opportunity: pitch a new initiative to the senior leadership team.

Maria's first instinct was: *"That's not for me. I'm not senior enough. I'll embarrass myself."*

But something shifted. She asked herself: *"What would the future version of me, five years from now, do?"*

She decided to go for it. She worked on her pitch obsessively. She practised in front of friends. She showed up, presented confidently, and blew them away.

Not only did the leadership team approve her idea, but they created a **new role** for her to lead it. She doubled her salary within a year. She now mentors other women on bold career moves.

All because she *thought big*, and backed it up with action.

---

## Simple Ways to Infuse Abundance into Your Career Today

### ✅ Reframe Rejection

Didn't get the job? Not a loss, a redirection. Something better is coming.

### ✅ Brag Better

Create a "confidence file" of wins, feedback, and results. Use it to reinforce your value.

### ✅ Give Generously

Share job leads, promote others' work, mentor someone. The energy you give *circulates back*.

### ✅ Ask Bigger Questions

Don't ask: "How can I survive this quarter?"
 Ask: "How can I scale my impact this year?"

### ✅ Play the Long Game

Plant seeds now, connections, content, learning, that will blossom later.

---

## Reflection: Career Abundance Check-In

1. Where am I thinking small in my work right now?

2. What am I afraid will happen if I start thinking bigger?

3. Who in my industry or circle models abundant career growth?

4. What's one bold move I could make this month to elevate my visibility or value?

---

## Takeaway

Your career is not something that *happens to you*. It's something you co-create, with your beliefs, actions, and vision.

Scarcity says:

> "Don't stand out."
> "Be grateful for what you have."
> "Play it safe."

Abundance says:

> "Be seen."
> "Go for more."

"There's room, and reward, for thinking
big."

The most expansive careers and businesses aren't built
by luck.
 They're built by people who *dared* to think differently,
then backed it with courage and consistency.

And that person? Can be you.

# Chapter 16: Abundance Habits & Daily Rituals

*"You will never change your life until you change something you do daily. The secret of your success is found in your daily routine." – John C. Maxwell*

---

## Abundance Is a Daily Practice, Not a One-Time Event

Mindset isn't something you set once and forget.
 It's like brushing your teeth, if you skip it too long, things start to decay.

That's why abundant thinkers don't just *believe* in abundance, they *live* it.

They build habits and rituals that reinforce the belief that there is enough time, enough opportunity, enough success, enough joy, for them and for others.

And they do it *every single day*.

You don't need to overhaul your life or wake up at 4am to think abundantly. But you *do* need to make consistent, conscious choices that shape your perspective and fuel your mindset.

Because abundance isn't just what you think, it's what you *repeat*.

---

## The Science of Habit and Mindset

Neuroscience tells us that our thoughts and behaviours create neural pathways. The more often you think or do something, the stronger those pathways become.

It's like walking through a forest: the more often you take the same path, the clearer and easier it becomes.

This means that every small, repetitive action, every morning affirmation, every journal entry, every generous act, **literally rewires your brain** for abundance.

And here's the best part: you don't need massive habits. You need *meaningful* ones.

---

## The "Day in the Life" of an Abundant Thinker

Let's paint a picture. Here's what a typical day might look like for someone who's anchored in abundance, someone who intentionally reinforces the mindset through simple, repeatable actions.

**Morning Rituals**

### ✅ Gratitude Upon Waking
Before checking their phone or rushing out of bed, they pause to silently name 3 things they're grateful for. This sets the emotional tone of the day: appreciation, not anxiety.

### ✅ Affirmations or Mantras
They repeat phrases like:

- "I am worthy of abundance."

- "There is more than enough."

- "I create value everywhere I go."

This isn't toxic positivity, it's *neural priming*. It tells the brain what to look for.

### ✅ Abundance-Focused Reading or Listening
While getting ready or commuting, they might listen to a podcast, audiobook, or YouTube video on mindset, wealth, or growth. It's like mental nourishment.

### ✅ Focused Intention-Setting
Before diving into work, they ask:
"What's one way I can think abundantly today?"
Then they write it down.

**Midday Microhabits**

### ☑ Generous Act
They compliment a colleague, share a resource, or support someone online, without expecting anything in return. Giving is an act of abundance.

### ☑ Pause and Breathe
They take 2 minutes to breathe deeply, stretch, or step outside. This reminds their nervous system: "There is time. I'm not behind. I'm okay."

### ☑ Decision Check
When a challenge arises, they ask:
"Am I responding from fear, or from faith in abundance?"

This one question re-centres everything.

**Evening Rituals**

### ☑ Reflection on Wins and Growth
Before bed, they jot down:

- What went well today

- What they're proud of

- One lesson they're taking forward

### ☑ Gratitude Round Two
They finish the day like they started, with appreciation.

Even if the day was hard, they *find the good*. That's abundance in action.

### ✓ Mental Rehearsal for Tomorrow

They visualise a positive outcome for the next day. This primes the subconscious to work *with* them overnight.

---

## Small Habits, Big Impact

You don't need to do all of the above. Start with *two or three* practices and build from there.

Here are some abundance-reinforcing habits to choose from:

### 📖 Morning Reading (10 minutes)

Read something that expands your thinking: a mindset book, a success story, a devotional. Feed your mind before the world fills it with noise.

### ✍ Journalling (5–15 minutes)

Try prompts like:

- "Where did I show up abundantly today?"

- "What opportunities am I ready to receive?"

- "How did I give freely this week?"

### 🐭 Daily Gratitude (2 minutes)

Write down 3 things you're grateful for. Make them specific and sincere. Gratitude rewires your brain to *see* abundance everywhere.

### 💬 Affirmations (spoken or written)

Use ones that resonate with your journey. Create your own if needed. Repetition builds belief.

### 🚶‍♂️ Movement and Nature

Walking, stretching, or simply being outside shifts your state. A calm, energised body supports an abundant mind.

### ☐ Mindful Input

Unfollow scarcity-based content online. Replace it with inspiring, practical, empowering voices. Your feed shapes your focus.

---

# Handling Setbacks Without Falling Back into Scarcity

Even the most abundant thinkers face bad days. But what sets them apart is how they *respond*.

Here's how to stay aligned when things go wrong:

## 1. Don't Spiral, Zoom Out

Instead of catastrophising, ask:
"What will this mean in six months?"
Often, what feels massive now becomes a footnote later.

## 2. Normalise Bumps

Abundant people know setbacks are part of the journey. They don't make them mean: "I'm not good enough." They make them mean: "I'm growing."

## 3. Return to Ritual

When shaken, go *back to the basics*: breathe, journal, repeat affirmations, call someone who believes in you. Rituals bring stability.

## 4. Choose Expansion Anyway

Even when tempted to shrink, take one small step forward.
Send the email. Share the idea. Say yes.

Momentum rebuilds abundance.

---

## Story: How Liam Rewired His Mindset with Rituals

Liam, a freelance videographer, used to wake up in stress and scramble. He'd check his phone, panic about leads, and compare himself to others on Instagram.

After reading a book on abundance, he started changing his mornings.

He woke up earlier. Wrote down three wins from the day before. Watched a 10-minute motivational video. Took a walk. Said three affirmations in the mirror, even when he didn't believe them.

Within a month, his energy shifted. He was calmer. More proactive. He reached out to pitch bigger clients, and started landing them.

He didn't "manifest success" overnight. But his rituals trained his mind to expect good things, and act accordingly.

Now, even when projects fall through or a pitch is rejected, he doesn't spiral. He returns to his rituals. He knows: *"I've built something solid inside me. And that's what counts."*

---

## Reflection: Designing Your Abundance Rituals

Grab a pen and answer:

1. What time of day do I feel most grounded and open?

2. What's one abundance habit I could add to my morning?

3. What's one habit I could use to close my day with gratitude or clarity?

4. How will I remind myself to return to these rituals when things feel hard?

---

## Takeaway

Your daily rituals are your declaration. They say:
"I believe in abundance, and I live like it."

You don't need to get it perfect. You just need to stay consistent.

Because small habits, repeated with intention, become powerful identities.
And your identity shapes your destiny.

Abundance is not a lucky break or a rare opportunity. It's something you *cultivate*. Every. Single. Day.

# Chapter 17: Leveraging Your Unique Value

*"Too many people overvalue what they are not and undervalue what they are." – Malcolm S. Forbes*

---

## You Are Not Lacking, You Are Loaded

Scarcity tells you a dangerous lie: *You're not enough.*
Not smart enough. Not qualified enough. Not talented enough.
And because you believe it, you stop trying. You don't ask. You don't speak up. You play small.

But the truth is this:

> **You don't need to become someone else to be valuable. You need to become more of yourself.**

Abundance isn't about being the loudest, the most polished, or the most famous. It's about recognising and releasing the unique gifts you already possess.

And here's the kicker: most people's greatest strengths are so natural to them, they overlook them completely.

That thing you do without thinking.
That insight you assume everyone has.
That life experience you've downplayed.

Those aren't trivial. They're treasure.

---

## Scarcity Says "Blend In." Abundance Says "Stand Out."

In a world obsessed with comparison, it's easy to think value is measured against others.

Scarcity thinking says:

- "If I can't do it like them, I shouldn't bother."

- "I need more qualifications before I'm credible."

- "Someone else is already doing it better."

- "My story isn't that special."

- "People like me don't succeed."

Abundance flips the script:

- "There's room for me, too."

- "My path is valid, even if it looks different."

- "No one else has my voice, my perspective, my blend of skills."

- "Someone is waiting for exactly what I offer."

The truth is, your power doesn't come from being like others.
 It comes from being *precisely* who you are.

---

## How to Identify Your Unique Value

Let's get practical. If you've been in the habit of downplaying your strengths, this is your moment to start recognising them.

Ask yourself:

### 1. What do people consistently thank me for?

Is it your listening skills? Your humour? Your ability to explain complex ideas simply?

Patterns of appreciation are a spotlight on your natural value.

### 2. What feels *easy* to me but hard to others?

We often dismiss our greatest gifts because they don't feel like "hard work." But ease doesn't mean lack of worth, it often means *mastery*.

### 3. What challenges have I overcome?

Your lived experiences, especially the painful ones, equip you to support, teach, or inspire others. There's gold in your story.

### 4. What topics could I talk about for hours?

Passion is often a clue to purpose. If something lights you up, chances are it energises others too.

### 5. What skills or traits have helped me thrive?

Think beyond job titles. Are you a connector? A problem solver? A calm presence in chaos? These are *portable powers*, valuable in any context.

---

## Story: From Invisible to Invaluable – How Tom Found His Edge

Tom was a warehouse worker in his mid-40s. He was reliable, consistent, and humble, but often felt invisible. He saw others climb the ladder while he stayed in place.

One day, a mentor at work asked him:

"What's something you're really good at that no one sees?"

Tom hesitated, then replied: "I'm good at noticing when things go wrong before they get worse. I've just always had an eye for it."

That offhand comment led to a conversation with his manager, who realised Tom had been preventing dozens of small disasters by catching inventory issues early.

They created a new role for him: **Quality and Efficiency Coordinator.** Within six months, the warehouse had cut errors by 40%. Tom trained others. His quiet skill became company-wide best practice.

Tom didn't learn a new trade. He *leveraged* what was already there.

And in doing so, he proved that value isn't always loud. Sometimes it's quiet, but deeply powerful.

---

## Building Confidence in What You Offer

Once you identify your value, you have to own it. And that's where scarcity likes to creep in.

Here's how to keep abundance at the forefront:

### ✓ Speak It Aloud

Say:

- "I'm really good at…"

- "One of my strengths is…"

- "People come to me for…"

Own your wins. Don't mumble them. Confidence isn't arrogance, it's accuracy.

### ✓ Collect Evidence

Keep a file, physical or digital, of kind messages, testimonials, results, feedback. When doubt strikes, read through your proof.

### ✓ Practice Value-Based Language

Instead of saying, "I just help small businesses," say, "I help small businesses grow their customer base through compelling brand messaging."

Specificity signals clarity, and clarity signals *value*.

### ✓ Get Feedback from Safe People

Sometimes we need a mirror. Ask trusted friends or colleagues:

> "What do you think I'm naturally gifted at?"
> You'll be surprised what others see in you that you've overlooked.

### ✅ Invest in Yourself

Take a course. Hire a coach. Start a project. Investing in yourself sends a message to your brain: *"I'm worth it."*

---

## From Self-Doubt to Self-Trust

Here's the real shift:

Scarcity asks:

> "Am I good enough?"

Abundance asks:

> "How can I serve more fully with what I already have?"

When you move from doubt to contribution, everything changes. You stop seeking validation. You start *offering value*.

And the world responds.

## Reflection: Unearthing Your Inner Wealth

Take 5 minutes to journal these:

1. Three compliments I've received repeatedly:

2. One life experience that's shaped my perspective:

3. One skill I take for granted that others find impressive:

4. One way I can use my gifts to help someone this week:

5. One belief I'm ready to upgrade about my worth:

---

## Takeaway

You are not behind.
 You are not too late.
 You are not missing the secret formula.

You are powerful. Not because of what you *might* become, but because of who you *already* are.

Abundance begins with acknowledging that your story, your strengths, your essence, have worth.

Own them. Share them. Build with them.

Because when you do, you don't just elevate your income or your confidence.
 You elevate your *impact*.

And that's real wealth.

# Chapter 18: Manifesting Abundance

*"What you think, you become. What you feel, you attract. What you imagine, you create." – Buddha*

---

## Manifestation Is More Than Magic Words

Let's get one thing clear: manifestation isn't about wishful thinking.
 It's not about closing your eyes, chanting "I am rich," and hoping the universe deposits a cheque.

It's about **clarity, belief, and action**, working together in alignment.

When people hear "manifestation," they often picture vision boards and affirmations. And yes, those are part of the process. But without *action*, they're just decoration.

Here's the truth:

> Manifestation is not magic. It's mindset with momentum.
>  It's belief *plus* behaviour.
>  It's tuning your mind to see opportunities, then *taking them*.

Abundant thinkers don't just hope. They prepare. They plan. They move.
And that's what brings their vision to life.

---

## The Law of Attraction (and What It Misses)

The Law of Attraction says:

> "Like attracts like."
> What you focus on, you draw into your life.

There's truth to that. Neuroscience backs it up, your brain filters information based on what you believe is possible. (It's called the Reticular Activating System.)

If you believe you're unlucky, you won't even *notice* the lucky breaks.
If you believe you're capable and worthy, you spot doors others walk past.

But here's where many go wrong:

They *only* focus on thoughts, forgetting action.

You can visualise your dream home every day, but if you never save, learn, invest, or network, it remains a Pinterest board fantasy.

Abundant manifestation is about creating mental *and* material conditions for success.

## How Beliefs + Behaviour Work Together

Let's break it down.

### 1. Beliefs Prime Your Brain

Your beliefs set the internal compass. They shape what you expect, and what you're prepared to receive.

If you believe there's always a way forward, you search differently.
 If you believe people are generous and open, you approach conversations with warmth.
 If you believe money flows easily to you, you stop apologising for charging your worth.

### 2. Behaviours Signal Readiness

Action tells the world, and yourself, that you're serious.

Want to write a book? Start writing.
 Want to earn more? Pitch, ask, promote, offer.
 Want love? Go where love lives. Be loving.

When belief and behaviour align, you send a powerful message:

> "I expect abundance, and I'm preparing for it."

And that's when opportunities, people, and results start appearing.

---

## The Tools of Practical Manifestation

These techniques aren't fluff, they're focus.

### 🔎 Vision Boards

Create a visual representation of your goals: income, lifestyle, relationships, freedom, health. It's not about being flashy, it's about clarity. Seeing your vision daily keeps it alive.

Tip: Use both *images* and *words*. Include how you want to *feel*, not just what you want to have.

### ▢▢ Scripting

Write a journal entry from your future self. Describe a day in your life once your vision is fulfilled. Be detailed. Write it in present tense:

> "I wake up in my dream home. I check the sales report, my business crossed £10,000 this month."

This "mental rehearsal" tells your subconscious: *this is real, this is happening.*

### 🎭 Mental Rehearsal

Elite athletes do this. So do top performers in every field.
They *see* themselves succeeding, before it happens.

Take five minutes a day to visualise:

- Walking confidently into the room

- Hitting "send" on the bold proposal

- Getting the call with good news

This activates the same brain circuits as actual experience. You're building readiness.

### 🗣️ Verbal Affirmations

Repeat statements that align with your vision. Not generic fluff, but intentional truths:

- "I am becoming the kind of person who handles wealth with ease."

- "Opportunities flow to me because I take bold action."

- "I'm building the habits that support my abundant life."

## Story: From Journal Page to Reality – Jade's Bold Vision

Jade was a primary school teacher who dreamed of opening her own tutoring centre. But scarcity kept her stuck:

> "Who would come to *my* centre?"
> "I don't have a business background."
> "It's too risky."

Still, she couldn't let go of the idea. So, she started small.

She created a vision board: photos of bright classrooms, smiling kids, invoices marked "Paid."

She journaled as if it had already happened:

> "Today, we signed up 12 new students. The parents said they love the calm, creative energy here."

She wrote it every morning before work. Then, she acted.

She spoke to colleagues. Took business courses online. Hired a mentor. Used her spare time to tutor one student, then two, then five.

Eighteen months later, Jade opened her centre. It was fully booked in the first month.

She credits her success not just to action, but to *alignment*, pairing vision with movement.

Jade says:

> "Writing it made me believe it. Acting on it made it real."

---

## Manifestation Mistakes to Avoid

Let's bust some myths:

### ✗ Waiting for "the universe" to deliver

Manifestation isn't passive. It's co-creation. Don't wait. *Work with the vision.*

### ✗ Obsessing over *how*

Focus on the *what* and *why*. Let the path unfold. Your job is to stay open, show up, and stay aligned.

### ✗ Doubting after delays

Just because it's slow doesn't mean it's wrong. Seeds take time. Keep nurturing.

**✗ Skipping the emotional work**

You can't out-manifest your self-worth. Heal. Release shame. Believe you're worthy.

---

## Reflection: Aligning Your Manifestation Practice

Grab your journal:

1.  What's one bold vision I haven't fully owned yet?

2.  What belief would I need to hold to make it real?

3.  What action can I take this week to show I'm ready?

4.  What daily ritual (vision board, scripting, affirmations) could help me focus?

---

## Takeaway

Manifestation is not woo, it's wiring.
It's belief applied through behaviour.
It's clarity met with commitment.

You don't manifest what you *want*, you manifest what you're *ready* to receive.

So make yourself ready.
 Be the person who holds the vision, takes the action, and lives the result.

Because when mindset meets movement, abundance follows.

# Chapter 19: Leaving Scarcity for Good

*"You can't get to abundance by holding onto scarcity."* –
*Brené Brown*

---

## Scarcity Doesn't Vanish, But You Can Outgrow It

Let's be honest: scarcity thinking doesn't completely disappear.

Even the most abundant people still feel moments of fear, doubt, or comparison.
 They still worry sometimes. They still question their worth.
 But here's the difference:

### They don't *live* there anymore.

They spot the scarcity story early.
 They pause.
 They choose differently.

That's what it means to *outgrow* scarcity.

Not to eliminate every fear forever, but to become the kind of person who can move *through* it, and back into abundance faster each time.

This chapter is about making that leap.
 The permanent shift away from survival mode, and into sustainable, expansive thinking.

---

## The Subtle Triggers of Scarcity (And How to Catch Them)

You might be making amazing progress, earning more, giving more, growing fast. But suddenly, you hit a moment. And it sneaks in:

- A friend shares good news, and you feel a flicker of envy.

- Your business has a quiet week, and panic starts rising.

- You see someone doing what you want to do, and feel like you're falling behind.

That's scarcity whispering:

> "There's not enough."
> "You're not enough."
> "This won't last."

To leave scarcity for good, you have to become **excellent at noticing** it.

Start looking out for these subtle cues:

## ⬜ Thought Triggers

"I can't afford that."
"They're more successful than me."
"This is too good to last."
"If I don't act fast, I'll miss out."

Challenge them with truth:

- *Is that really true? Or just an old belief resurfacing?*

- *What else could be true right now?*

## 💬 Language Triggers

Watch how you talk, especially about money, time, and opportunity.
Do you say things like:

- "I'm broke."

- "That's way out of my league."

- "I never catch a break."

- "It's just not meant for people like me."

Flip the script:

- "I'm learning to handle money well."

- "I'm working toward that level."

- "I create my own luck."

- "If it's possible for them, it's possible for me."

### ⚧ **Behavioural Triggers**

Notice how you act when you feel uncertain.
Do you shrink? Withdraw? Hoard? Avoid?

Instead: pause and ask, *"What would abundant me do right now?"*

---

## Staying Abundant in Tough Times

It's easy to think abundantly when things are going well.
But the real test? When life gets messy. Slow.
Unexpected.

That's when your mindset gets built, or broken.

Here are three principles for staying grounded in abundance when things get hard:

## 1. Zoom Out

When panic hits, scarcity zooms in on the problem. It magnifies the issue and blocks solutions.

Abundance zooms out and says:

- "This is one moment, not the whole story."

- "I've overcome worse before."

- "This setback has something to teach me."

Perspective is power.

## 2. Resource Over React

Instead of asking, "Why is this happening to me?" ask, "What resources do I have right now?"

Think:

- Who could I reach out to?

- What skill could I offer?

- What option haven't I explored yet?

Scarcity fixates on lack. Abundance searches for leverage.

### 3. Rituals Over Emotion

When emotions run high, stick to the habits that anchor you.

- Journal.

- Breathe.

- Move your body.

- Say the affirmation.

- Read the book.

- Do the small action.

You don't need to feel confident to act. But acting abundantly restores confidence.

---

## Story: From Scarcity to Stability – Natalie's Long Game

Natalie was a single mum in her late 30s, raising two boys and juggling a low-income job. Money was always tight. Her mindset was shaped by early experiences of instability and shame.

She often said things like:

- "We're not like those families."

- "I just need to survive this week."

- "I don't want to get my hopes up."

Then she stumbled on a podcast episode about abundance. It wasn't magic, it didn't change everything overnight. But it planted a seed.

She began reading. Journalling. Writing down what she was grateful for.
 She opened a savings account, even if she could only add £5 a week.

She started a side hustle, offering childcare and tutoring in her community. It grew slowly. Then faster. She invested in a business course. She started believing she had value.

Years later, she was earning double her old salary, on her own terms. But more than the income, it was her mindset that changed.

Natalie says:

> "Scarcity still shows up sometimes. But now I see it for what it is, a story. I've rewritten the ending."

Her transformation wasn't a quantum leap. It was a series of tiny shifts, made daily, over time.
And that's how you leave scarcity for good.

---

## Your Mindset Evolution Is a Journey

Here's what abundant people know:

- You won't wake up one day "cured" of scarcity.

- You'll still have moments of fear.

- But they won't define you anymore.

Instead of spiralling, you'll *notice*.
Instead of freezing, you'll *act*.
Instead of comparing, you'll *contribute*.

Every time you choose to respond differently, you stretch your mindset wider.
And that stretch creates space, for growth, income, joy, love, and *legacy*.

---

## Reflection: Your Expansion Map

1. When was the last time I felt scarcity sneak in? How did I respond?

2. What's one old belief I'm finally ready to let go of for good?

3. What's a new abundant habit or response I can commit to in those moments?

4. Who have I become in the past year, and what does that say about what's possible next?

---

## Takeaway

You don't "beat" scarcity by force.
You outgrow it, through self-awareness, self-trust, and daily abundant choices.

The old fear-based version of you may still whisper.
But now, you've got new tools. A stronger voice. A clearer path.

The fact you've come this far means you've already started your transformation.
This isn't theory for you anymore, it's *truth lived out*.

And the more you walk this road, the more you realise:

**Abundance isn't the destination. It's who you become on the way.**

# Chapter 20: Creating a Legacy of Abundance

*"You can't take your wealth with you. But you can leave behind something far greater: the mindset that created it." – Alex Carter*

---

## Abundance Is Bigger Than You

You've done the work.

You've shifted your thinking.
You've challenged old beliefs.
You've made decisions not from fear, but from faith in your own worth and potential.

But here's the ultimate truth about abundance:

> **It's not real until it's shared.**
> **It's not finished until it outlives you.**

The most abundant people don't just earn more, live better, or enjoy success.
They pass it on, through ideas, systems, habits, and values.

They leave behind more than money. They leave behind *mindset*.

Because that's the real legacy.
 One that multiplies, evolves, and empowers generation after generation.

---

## What Legacy Really Means (It's Not Just Money)

When most people hear "legacy," they think of wealth. Trust funds. Wills. Property.

And yes, *material legacy* matters. Especially if you've built something substantial and want to ensure it benefits your family or community.

But legacy is also:

- Teaching your kids to think expansively

- Giving your team the confidence to take risks

- Inspiring others to live boldly

- Funding ideas that shape the world

- Creating tools, teachings, or systems that keep serving long after you're gone

The most powerful legacies come from ordinary people who made an *intentional choice* to plant seeds they might never see grow.

That's abundance thinking in its highest form.

---

## Teaching Abundance to Others

Want to raise abundant children? Lead an abundant team? Uplift your community?

Don't just share money. Share *mindset*.

Here's how to model abundance to those around you:

### ☐ Talk About Possibility, Not Just Problems

Scarcity constantly points out what's wrong. Abundance focuses on what's possible.

Instead of: "We can't afford that," try:

- "Let's figure out how to make that happen."

- "What would it take to achieve that?"

- "What skill or idea could help us get there?"

### ☐☐ Teach Tools, Not Dependence

Give your children or mentees the skills to generate, save, and invest, don't just hand over results. Help them build *capacity*, not just comfort.

### 💬 Celebrate Growth, Not Just Outcome

Whether it's a child's effort, a team's experimentation, or a peer's bold move, praise the *abundant action*, not just the win.

This teaches people to value *courage over certainty*, and to see failure as part of expansion.

### ⚰ Share Stories of Change

Talk about your own mindset journey. How you used to think. What you've unlearned. Where you still struggle. Transparency is powerful.

You're not just teaching success. You're showing what's *possible to evolve*.

---

## Building Systems That Outlast You

One-off acts are generous. But systems are what create sustainable legacy.

Ask yourself:

- Can I document what I know, so others can learn from it?

- Can I automate or outsource parts of my work so it can run without me?

- Can I create scholarships, funds, or donations that continue over time?

- Can I mentor others to take over what I've built?

Legacy isn't about being irreplaceable.
It's about being *repeatable*.

The best systems don't make you the hero. They make you the *bridge* to something greater.

---

## Generational Wealth and Philanthropy

If you've built financial abundance, you have a chance to do something most people never get to:

**Change the trajectory of your bloodline, or someone else's.**

That might mean:

- Creating trusts or investment accounts for your children or grandchildren

- Buying property to pass down

- Supporting your parents or siblings

- Donating to causes that reflect your values

- Endowing scholarships or funding local initiatives

- Teaching others how to grow wealth from any starting point

But the key isn't *just* giving. It's **educating alongside the giving**.
 Without mindset, money can be misused or misinterpreted.

With mindset, money becomes a *tool for vision*.

---

## Story: Two Legacies, Two Outcomes

Let's contrast two stories.

**Legacy #1: The Lottery Winner**

David won £2 million in a lottery. He bought cars, holidays, houses. He gave generously to friends and family, often out of guilt or obligation.

Within five years, the money was gone.
 No investments. No savings. No structure.
 His relationships were strained. His mental health suffered.

Why? Because the *money outpaced the mindset*.

**Legacy #2: The Baker Who Taught**

Fatima ran a local bakery for 30 years. She wasn't wealthy in the traditional sense, but she trained over 20 young people from her community in business, leadership, and self-belief.

When she retired, one of her former apprentices expanded the bakery into a catering business. Another opened a food truck. One became a motivational speaker.

Fatima's legacy wasn't the money she left, it was the *mindset and model* she handed down.

Abundance doesn't require millions. It requires *multiplication*.

## Reflection: Designing Your Abundant Legacy

Take some time to journal:

1. Who do I want to impact long after I'm gone?

2. What values or lessons do I want to pass down?

3. What systems, tools, or teachings could I create?

4. What money (or mindset) habits do I need to model more consistently?

And most importantly:

5. What would a legacy rooted in abundance, not fear, look like for me?

---

## Takeaway

You are not just here to *earn*.
You are here to *extend*.
To take the wealth, mental, emotional, financial, that you've built, and *send it forward*.

That's what legacy is: not hoarding, but handing down. Not control, but contribution.

Your abundant life becomes even more powerful when it becomes *part of someone else's breakthrough*.

So write the will. Teach the skill. Share the story. Plant the seed.

> Because your greatest success won't just
> be what you built.
> It will be who you *lifted* while you did it.

# Conclusion: Your Abundant Life Awaits

*"Abundance is not something we acquire. It is something we tune into." – Wayne Dyer*

---

## You've Already Started

If you've made it to this point in the book, something profound has already happened:

You're no longer unaware.
You're no longer operating purely on default.
You've started thinking differently.
And that's everything.

Because abundance doesn't begin with the numbers in your bank account, the titles on your CV, or the square footage of your home.

It begins the moment you decide:

> "I will no longer live my life in fear of not having, being, or doing enough."

You've made that decision.
And now? Everything expands from here.

---

# From Scarcity Thinking to Abundant Living

Let's quickly revisit the core shift you've made on this journey:

- From **fear** to **possibility**

- From **competition** to **collaboration**

- From **lack** to **leverage**

- From **reacting** to **creating**

- From **surviving** to **thriving**

You've learned how scarcity shows up, subtly and overtly, in your thoughts, language, spending, relationships, and decisions.
 You've seen how to spot it, challenge it, and replace it with truth.

More importantly, you've been equipped with tools:

✓ Affirmations and visualisation

✓ Gratitude and generosity

✓ Identity work and belief rewiring

✓ Practical financial strategies

✓ Daily abundance rituals

✓ Long-term decision frameworks

This is not surface-level motivation. This is rewiring the *core* of how you see yourself and the world.

---

## Take the First (Small) Step, Today

You don't need to overhaul your life in a day. You just need to act *in alignment*.

Here are a few small yet mighty steps you could take right now:

- **Say yes** to an opportunity you'd normally overthink

- **Compliment yourself**, out loud

- **Send the message** or email you've been hesitating on

- **Start the journal** where you script your abundant future

- **Make one brave financial decision**, even if it's saving £10

- **Tell someone you believe in them** (and mean it)

- **Write down five things** you're grateful for, immediately

- **Change one sentence** in your internal dialogue from lack to truth

Small steps compound. The sooner you start, the faster the shift takes root.

---

## Choose to Live This Way for Life

This is not a 30-day challenge. It's a lifetime commitment.

Because life will throw curveballs.
 Scarcity will try to sneak back in, especially in tough times.

But now, you know how to return to centre.
 You've got the mindset. The habits. The language. The tools.

And you've got a choice:

> Keep growing.
>  Keep stretching.

Keep saying yes to the kind of life where there's more than enough, of everything that matters.

Abundance isn't a destination you reach. It's a way you choose to live.

---

## A Final Word From Alex

I wrote this book not because I've always thought abundantly, but because I *didn't*.
I know what it feels like to live under the weight of scarcity.
To feel like there's not enough time, money, opportunity, talent, or space for you.

But I also know what's on the other side of that story.

Peace.
Confidence.
Generosity.
Ease.
Expansion.

You've already started rewriting your story. Now go *live* it.

Abundance isn't waiting around the corner.

**It's already here, inside you.**

Your abundant life isn't just possible.
It's *ready*.

Go meet it.

**Thank You for Reading.**

If this book offered you clarity, calm, or a shift in how you see the world, I'd be truly grateful if you took a moment to share your thoughts in a **short Amazon review**.

Your reflection helps other readers discover timeless ideas that still matter today and keeps the philosophy alive for those who seek it.

Your words keep wisdom moving forward.

# THE WEALTH SERIES

**Alex Carter** is an internationally recognised wealth mindset coach, financial empowerment speaker, and New York Times bestselling author. With over 20 years of experience in personal finance, entrepreneurship, and personal development, Alex has helped thousands transform their financial futures, not by chasing money, but by mastering their mindset.

Website: **edenrootpress.com**
Instagram: **edenroot.press**

How to Be Wealthy Mindset

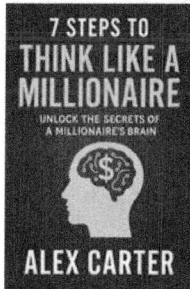

7 Steps to Think Like a Millionaire

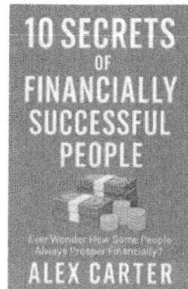

10 Secrets of Financially Successful People

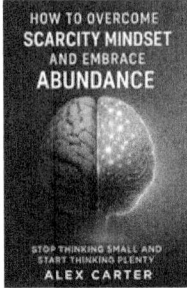

How to Overcome a
Scarcity Mindset and
Embrace Abundance

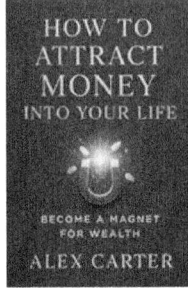

How to Attract
Money into Your Life

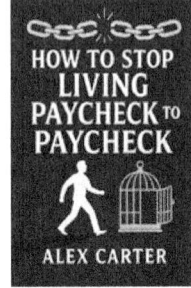

How to Stop Living
Paycheck to
Paycheck

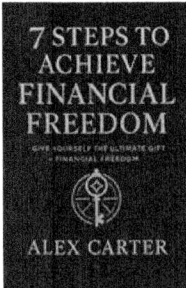

7 Steps to Achieve
Financial Freedom

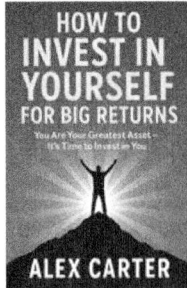

How to Invest in
Yourself for Big
Returns

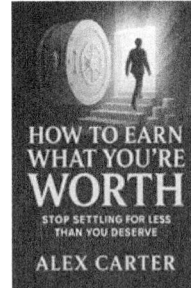

How to Earn What
You're Worth

How to Overcome
Fear of Success and
Prosper

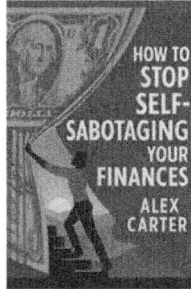

How to Stop Self-
Sabotaging Your
Finances

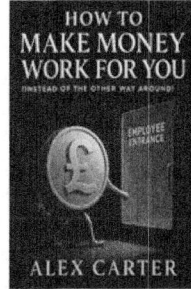

How to Make Money
Work for You

How to Build Wealth on Any
Income

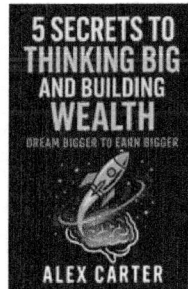

5 Secrets to Thinking Big and
Building Wealth

Printed in Dunstable, United Kingdom